T0277347

Praise for
Shaping the Future of Education

"I've just opened your book and need to force myself to look away! After each paragraph I find myself saying, 'Yes, yes, yes!' I hope and pray your book is welcomed with open arms. As I read, I think back to our own local school system (Todd County) voted worst in our state . . . we desperately need this type of transformation in our systems!"

—Dr. Nora Antoine, professor and board of education member for the Rosebud School District

"Educating each child based on individual achievement, passion, and potential has always been a challenge for schools. Utilizing the exponential growth in technology and artificial intelligence over the past few years, Nolan and Leah have created a blueprint to differentiated success unlike any that I have seen in my 20+ years in education."

—Rory Peacock, K–12 educator

Shaping *the* Future *of* Education

Shaping
the Future
of
Education

THE ExoDexa Manifesto

Nolan Bushnell and
Dr. Leah Hanes

GREENLEAF
BOOK GROUP PRESS

Published by Greenleaf Book Group Press
Austin, Texas
www.gbgpress.com

Distributed by Greenleaf Book Group

For ordering information or special discounts for bulk purchases, please contact Greenleaf Book Group at PO Box 91869, Austin, TX 78709, 512.891.6100.

Design and composition by Greenleaf Book Group and Kim Lance
Cover design by Greenleaf Book Group and Kim Lance

Publisher's Cataloging-in-Publication data is available.

Print ISBN: 979-8-88645-005-7

eBook ISBN: 979-8-88645-006-4

Audiobook ISBN: 979-8-88645-007-1

To offset the number of trees consumed in the printing of our books, Greenleaf donates a portion of the proceeds from each printing to the Arbor Day Foundation. Greenleaf Book Group has replaced over 50,000 trees since 2007.

Printed in the United States of America on acid-free paper

23 24 25 26 27   10 9 8 7 6 5 4 3 2 1

First Edition

According to UNICEF, over 600 million children
and adolescents are unable to reach minimum proficiency levels in
reading and math, even though two thirds of them are in school.

This book is dedicated to the children left behind.

Contents

Foreword by Jon Kraft   xi

Introduction: This Book Is a Manifesto   1

1 Why This Book?   13

2 Our Primary Goals   39

3 Lifelong Interest Comes with Curiosity   55

4 Instill Optimism and Enthusiasm   75

5 The Roles of Staff, Mentors, and the Student's Home   95

6 Cultivate Enthusiasm and Creativity   119

7 Target Individual Interests and Schedules   139

8 Sharing User Experiences   165

9 Nolan's Blueprint for ExoDexa Schools   221

Conclusion   239

Appendix: Topics for Future Study   *241*

Index   *245*

About the Authors   *255*

by Jon Kraft

t was a tremendous honor for me to be asked by Nolan Bushnell, the father of video games, and Dr. Leah Hanes, a lifelong educator and entrepreneur, to write the foreword to their book, *Shaping the Future of Education*.

My first memory of Nolan was circa 2002. I had just started Pandora Media, and Nolan was a guest speaker at the Garage Technology Ventures annual startup conference. I was in awe of his larger-than-life persona and his irreverence toward the industry that had come to dominate my world and most of Silicon Valley: venture capital. That irreverence did not come from a place of arrogance nor any disregard for the powerful kingmakers of Sand Hill Road. Rather, from the impressionable perspective of a 29-year-old entrepreneur, it came from his passion and belief in the inevitability and unstoppable positivity of great ideas and great work.

I met Leah a decade later when she was running the Two Bit Circus Foundation and their now-famous STEAM Carnival. One of my startups, Thrively, had set up a station at the STEAM Carnival to engage with children and families and spread awareness of our platform. While Thrively is now in over 100,000 classrooms, back then we were just getting our footing, and we loved what Leah had done with both the Carnival and the Foundation as a whole. In partnership with Nolan's son, Brent Bushnell, she had helped make Two Bit Circus an iconic organization for unleashing in kids a relentless creativity and a deep passion for learning through their programs, events, and "Maker Spaces."

It's wonderful that Nolan and Leah have collaborated on this book, and I'm delighted that Nolan has started to direct his energy and passion into one of the most important domains we can impact as innovators: education. *Shaping the Future of Education* is in varying parts passion, vision, pragmatism, and futurism. It features vividly painted case studies to illustrate challenges, as well as detailed proposals for ways to modernize and transform the educational experience for everyone. It pops off the page as part instruction manual for impacting the current educational structure and part strategic road map to the future. Discerning which idea falls into what category is (intentionally, I believe) left to the discretion of the reader. What better way to spark debate and dialogue than to tease a bit of futurism and disruption, mixed with a series of pragmatic, near-term proposals for change, and allow people to engage in discussion about what is possible and when?

Because of the strength of Nolan and Leah's vision, it's easy to feel as if you've stumbled across the secret manuscript of a full-blown educational manifesto, with hints of revolution teased in the margins. But revolution is not what they're calling for. Nolan and Leah understand at a deep level the critical role that schools, and specifically teachers, play in developing students' minds. However, they also recognize that the current structure of schools leads to undue burdens and responsibilities for teachers that fall well outside of their core passions and skill sets: teaching and inspiring children.

As change accelerates in our world, the ideas of this book are less about revolution and more about providing a peek into the pockets of innovation that we will inevitably see in education, some starting now, and others developing over the next decade or two. In fact, some key innovations that they discuss are already taking shape before our eyes.

Two Bit Circus has been working for years on integrating Maker Spaces into schools throughout both the Los Angeles Unified School District and Dallas Independent School District. With ExoDexa, Nolan and Leah's new EdTech start-up, a number of districts will soon be embarking on the kind of personalization and gamification of lessons that Chapter 7 of the book discusses. And perhaps most ubiquitous of all near-term changes, AI is exploding everywhere you turn.

At its core, the book asks some fundamental questions: "What if we could personalize the learning experience for all kids?" and "What if we made a concerted effort to build optimism and enthusiasm into our curricula?" And then it also asks more provocative questions: "What if we encourage our kids to start businesses while in school?" or even, "What if we drastically reduce the structure within a school day?"

But central to everything that Nolan and Leah express in these pages is the critical role of teachers as *mentors* who, leveraging technology and creative spaces, *educate* and *inspire* more than they wrangle and discipline. *Shaping the Future of Education* paints a picture of a new era, which, with the help of tech and some creative thinking, can completely transform both the enthusiasm that children bring to school each day and the depth of knowledge and skills that they take away from it each year.

Enjoy!

This Book Is a Manifesto

These pages constitute a blueprint for changing the world through the way we educate our children and everyone throughout life. Make no mistake, this book is a recruiting document. If we change education, we can change the world!

Yes, that's a bold statement, and this is a bold undertaking, but it's one we believe is both essential and inevitable. The way we have been doing education for the last century has only worked for a handful of students. We want something for everyone, knowing that everyone is different. And we want you to join us in this mission.

A COMPARISON OF TWO CLASSROOMS

Let us start our story with a tale of two students in two very different classrooms. "Pat" is in a typical classroom, the kind of school most of us attended, sent our children to, and perhaps teach in today. "Sam," on the other hand, attends what we envision as the "school of the future."

Pat's Experience

Pat sits down for 90 minutes and slogs through math class preparing to take the test. When the teacher isn't looking, the students are catching glimpses of Instagram or Snapchat or checking their text messages. So is Pat. If they can, they play games, take naps at their desk, whatever they can get away with while the teacher is giving the lecture.

Most of the kids were up late playing the latest release of their favorite video game so that nap feels necessary. Pat manages five- and six-minute naps when the teacher is busy at the front of the room with another student. In 90 minutes the bell is going to ring, and Pat is going to pack up that backpack and head to the next class, the second lecture of the day.

Some of the students have been able to focus, but not Pat. That was true for a little less than a third of the class. The rest are in their own heads working out something. About half of this group is thinking about school and deadlines, the rest are thinking about the next level in their favorite game, the next party, date, film, whatever gets their attention. They sit through the next 90 minutes struggling to concentrate.

Lunch is loud and energetic. There is a lot of energy in the room. Pat sits with the same group of students every day. Students know who belongs in which group relatively quickly in this school.

After lunch the pressure is on. The competition among students is high, and grades and rewards make a difference. Everyone becomes a little less friendly and a lot more secretive. None of the students want to share ideas and risk being copied, so competition brings the need for secrecy. When Pat needs help, there are teachers around, but it's better to watch YouTube videos in isolation so you don't risk giving away any of the details of your project. Sometimes Pat's parents hire a tutor to help, but that is expensive, and the family doesn't have a lot of extra money for educational backup.

Sam's Experience

Sam and a group of energetic kids show up to the school ready to engage. Sam, who was up late playing a video game, is going to the nap room to catch an extra hour of sleep before settling into the day's work. Sam wakes up from a nap refreshed and ready to take on the day. The sleeping pods are available for sign-up as needed. No questions or judgments. If you need a nap, you take one. That has helped Sam through more than one difficult day.

Instead of dreading a math test or leaning over to copy a neighbor's paper, Sam eagerly pulls out the school iPad and fires up the game. Sam made it to level 6 this week. That tells us a lot. What Sam missed is the fact that there was a test buried in that game, which Sam took and passed without knowing one was being administered.

The teachers in these classrooms are there when needed. The system alerts the teacher when a student is struggling with something so they can intervene before frustration becomes overwhelming.

Sam has called on the teacher, who feels more like a mentor than a teacher, to help sort through thoughts and ideas. Sam and the other students are sitting in groups, and some are in cubicles working on their own. Most of the time they are collaborating with fellow students or mentoring younger students in a game or project. Sam says it helps anchor the learning. Sam has a good time working with the younger group, remembering how cool the older kids once seemed.

At lunch break the students are offered nutritious options for their meals. All the rationale for the meal is in their menu, tied to their life-sciences course, but no one asks about that. The kids have an app they engage to create their ideal meal plan, which leaves room for "entertainment eating," and they know the difference. They also know how to manage their own meal system for their highest levels of performance. Calories aren't counted for weight, they are counted for energy. Sam has always known that students in this school have the freedom to choose what to eat. Sometimes only a coffee or a candy bar is needed to get an energy boost.

The difference for Sam and the other students is that they will track and understand their body's messages about each meal choice. Sam believes that food is fuel and should also be immensely enjoyable to the taste buds. Although nutrition was never a subject high on Sam's radar, it now seems like a possible career, perhaps as a high-end chef. Sam is 15 years old and would be a sophomore in a typical high school, but Sam is close to completing a full course load and is now thinking about entrepreneurial projects that could be part of the next school year, for example, a food truck.

Sam and the others are energetic in physical education (PE) class. The game (the place where learning is buried) has helped them understand the importance of aerobic and anaerobic movement. They track themselves for optimum output—both physical and mental. Sam has never been a fan of PE. But here it's a little different than at any previous school Sam has attended. At this campus it is about movement and heart rate. Caring about sports is a personal choice; it's not required. Sam chose dancing for the physical education class but wasn't comfortable dancing in front of anyone. Not a problem, Sam can monitor any movement at home and log it onto the app to chart progress.

Art class is similarly self-directed with an artist/faculty member functioning as a sounding board or facilitator. Each student is in charge of their artistic expression. The school has supplied enough raw materials for any student to find an art form that helps them with focus, expression, and voice. Sam discovered a talent for sculpting and a keen interest in voice and music. Sam will be one to watch.

Sam loves the group projects. Most of the students collaborate within and outside of their group. At weekly meetings each of the groups present their progress and receive feedback from each other. The atmosphere is one of support. Competition may exist, but no one is focused on beating or outdoing anyone else. This group has the mindset that when one group does something well, it will positively affect other groups. They motivate each other and cheer each other on.

Sam also has a support system that goes beyond the project group. Tutors are available to help with group projects and individual needs; they are experts in their fields and are generous with their time and expertise. Sam is so far into this process that any and all advice is considered. The motivation to dig deeper comes from within, because Sam is looking for information not validation.

FOLLOWING OUR CONVERSATION

Given those two options, which do you think a middle school student would choose? High school students? We were all those students once, and I have no question about the choice the majority would make. What we've presented here is not a collection of random ideas but a collection of workable solutions. Every bold concept is lifted from the available research. If it has been proven and tested by rigorous and capable scientists, does that mean it's also *bold*? Not always. So think of this as an execution document. How do we use all this current research in a friendly and cohesive way? A way that does not break the bank? And how do we further document and prove that our ideas work?

We start with this book. Think of it as a conversation between two speakers: a serial tech entrepreneur, Nolan Bushnell, who is the father of the video game industry; and an educator, myself, who is a leader in the field of STEAM education and environmental stewardship.

Later in this book you will find a blueprint for how we propose to change the world through changing the way we educate. We'll show you what we mean by workable solutions.

If not now, when? If not us, who?

THE AUTHORS

Tech as a sector has disrupted and changed our world, and it has its own unique culture and language. Ideas from this world can be of tremendous benefit to educators, but they require some degree of contextualization for the rest of us in order to be understood and applied. In order to give that context, we will provide more background on the nature of Nolan's proposal for the changes required in education through his well-considered contribution to this text.

Nolan writes not in the form of a thesis or essay, but in the form of a **User Story**. In the technology world, user stories are descriptions of a system or feature from the perspective of the user of the product.

USER STORIES: GRAY TEXT BOXES ARE IN NOLAN'S VOICE.

The first tech-world cultural difference we encounter is in the use of the word "product." We educators would rarely think of education as a product. It's not to be bought and sold according to consumer demand. It's the mission, the efforts of our joint passion for building the next generation through engagement in their learning experience. However, a product in the context of a tech company is whatever the company's end goal is to create, whether this is software, a service, or anything else that is designed to meet a need and create value for a group of people.

A document such as the one Nolan has written is intended to lay out the ideal experience of the end user, describe how the product meets that experience, and guide creative and technical contributors to put forward the strategies and tactics that will be used to achieve those goals.

There is one central technique you will see used again and again in this book: imagining how the end user interacts with the product. You may have heard that "the design process begins with empathy." The first step is to build profiles of hypothetical users, based on research. Then these profiles are used to imagine how a particular subset of hypothetical users would interact with the product from beginning to end: the user journey.

What needs would bring them to the product? What might their experience be like while using it? What end results would they achieve for themselves? When you see stories about students or teachers sprinkled throughout this work, keep in mind that these are not always accounts of things that have happened. They are often journeys of imagination, which help the builders of the product work in such a way as to later achieve those desired results in real life. These users tend to be composite characters based on information gained from a wide variety of interviews, human-interest pieces, and academic research.

In the words of Carl Sagan, "dreams are maps," and the stories you will find in this book are the dreams we will use to map our way to a better future for education.

So, bearing all that in mind, what you will experience in the coming chapters is a conversation between a tech entrepreneur with a vision of education and an educator with a lens on the foundations and practice of that vision.

Who Is Nolan?

Most people between 20 and 50 know Nolan as the single biggest architect of their childhoods. Many people over 70 (i.e., their parents) blame him for their kids' addiction to video games. For the record, Nolan Bushnell is best known for founding Atari and Chuck E. Cheese and being the first person to hire Steve Jobs. A lesser-known facet of his history of innovation is that he launched one of the earliest tech incubators, the first in Silicon Valley. There he had the vision to experiment with ideas and grow the best. These experiments led to the creation of technologies that are now common but were then ahead of their time, such as the precursor to today's GPS-based automotive navigation systems and digitized maps. Nolan saw the world and dreamed of how it could be better, inspiring an entire generation of Silicon Valley entrepreneurs.

Nolan has been thinking about the educational power of video games since the first moment video games twinkled into existence with his creation of the very first one, Computer Space, and then Pong.

When Nolan left Atari in the late 1980s, the first thing he did was create an educational computer camp for kids. Since then he's never stopped ideating, experimenting, and dreaming about ways to improve education using the power of video games, and this book is the fruit of that lifelong obsession.

Nolan says, "I immediately found that video games were satisfying to kids; you can even call them addicting, because they represent a very tight, sensitive, and thrilling environment. Everything that we've thought about traditional school subjects can be set to games."

Nolan shared his story of founding Atari in his previous book, *Finding the Next Steve Jobs*. In that book he also confirms what he has long believed: that we learn more from our setbacks than from our successes. He is candid about how that perspective in life helped shape his approach to both games and education.

He says, "We build challenges into the games so there are setbacks and failures that the student learns to navigate. This is how to nurture grit and help students understand what one can do to find their way to the other side of those difficult and informative experiences."

Nolan also has "Dad" experience on his resume, with three girls and five boys, all of them now exceptional adults. Clearly, as the father to eight kids, he's comfortable being challenged.

Who Is Leah?

For the last decade, I have worked exclusively in education. First, as executive director and now CEO of the Two Bit Circus Foundation, I have developed and conducted professional development that encourages teachers to adopt project- and problem-based learning in an effort to move teachers from lecture-style teaching to a more engaging, hands-on format. In the case of the Two Bit Circus Foundation we also add an environmental stewardship message to our programs and projects by using upcycled materials rescued from manufacturers' waste streams. We have done this in hundreds of schools and have built 200-plus STEAM Lab Makerspaces (SLMs) filled with material and standards-aligned project books for teachers to help them work with their students to prototype their ideas.

Also during this time I worked with industry experts and educators like Russell Billings, former educator with NASA and STEM educator, and Darlene Torrez from the Department of Innovation of the Los Angeles Unified School District (LAUSD), to design the STEAM curriculum. I presided over the design of this curriculum and introduced the program into the LAUSD, one of the world's largest and most complex school systems. This was and is a STEAM (science, technology, engineering, arts, and math) program that engages children and teaching staff. In our ongoing relationship we train their teachers to engage the students in standards-aligned, project-based learning.

We then set up a successful program to install those SLMs into other unified school districts around the country. We design curriculum, maintain the labs with fresh materials, and, most importantly, offer professional development to teachers interested in moving from traditional teaching styles to learning by doing. We have trained hundreds of LA Unified teachers, under the auspices of the district administration, for the last seven years. We have done this in dozens of school districts in California and now also in Nashville, Tennessee. These SLMs are hubs of inquiry, exploration, and collaboration.

But my story as an educator doesn't start with "I was doing so well at everything that I decided to stop, evaluate, and redirect my life into higher education." No, as Nolan noted earlier, struggle is where the learning takes place. My story as an educator starts with "things were no longer working for me and I needed a change." I had been in the entertainment industry for a couple of decades. It was where I had developed many of my entrepreneurial skills; I had a few great successes and a few spectacular failures. I had learned a great deal from those failures and was considering my options. Among those options was finishing a PhD and teaching at a local university, which I did for a few years. It was a considerable change from my earlier years in education, when I was a preschool teacher.

Our ability to face failures and find a lesson without seeing the experience as defeat is essential to the long-term success of a project, an education, or a career. Few have made it to the top of a profession or an industry without firsthand experience with failure. My way of adjusting was to follow a lifelong passion for education.

Education was a passion I couldn't afford to follow as a young woman. I was a mother at 21 and a single mom by 25. I needed to make more money than I was earning as a nursery school teacher. So, rather than finish a degree and teach, I made choices about work rather than career in order to make a difference in my income. I often joke with friends that it took me 30 years to finish my homework. For those years I was a businesswoman and considered by those who knew me to be fairly successful.

I also bring that business and entrepreneurial experience to this discussion. I come with informed questions about education from a variety of personal perspectives, including as a mother of two children who completed their education in the public school system, first in Canada, followed by middle and high school in Los Angeles. As a community member, I mourn the reality of what I see in the physical buildings we send our children to year after year. Those buildings sometimes look more like detention centers than schoolyards. Nolan's ideas about the physical building and its use for students are both intriguing and ripe for research, as you'll see in the coming chapters.

So many of the issues I run into in the schools we serve punctuate the need for change from the physical experience of the building and schoolyard to the way we operate in the classroom.

Educators are our rock stars. They spend every day nurturing and inspiring our children. This book is our offering to those educators as well as every parent, community member, or business leader looking for ideas for implementing new systems in a world that may not be ready for, or embrace, change.

CHAPTER 1

Why This Book?

N olan has been talking about education and has been passionate about what could be done with a reorganized system of educating, and he took the time to write about it. Then he asked me to work with him to complete the book. He asked me to consider his proposal for a school of the future and offer an academic view from someone working in the system as it exists.

During these last dozen years working in education, I've become an advocate for a revolution in the way we educate our children. Nolan has taken the time to explain how that revolution could look and what it would offer students and educators. We are not alone in this desire. Others also see the need to bring about major change. But few have created a blueprint for that change the way Nolan has in this book.

The disruption caused by the global pandemic in 2020 offered the possibility of just such a revolution. Students have lost time, instruction, and the ability to gather with other students to explore ideas. But many have fought to get back to school as usual. If that is what we do, we will all have missed a significant opportunity to positively impact this generation with the promise of change. In contrast, if change is done properly, we will see progress in the trajectory of our educational system for these students and for future generations.

Nolan approaches this need for change from a business perspective and is healthily skeptical about the way it will be approached in education:

> Usually in a business you say, "What's the objective of this business?" In education it's to educate good citizens who can be gainfully employed and to do it efficiently. Don't waste their time. That would be the design goals of the school system. But to date, the goal seems instead to be all about protecting the performance curve and maintaining the status quo.

Are current schools meeting this objective? Sadly, we have to say the answer is largely, no.

At the Two Bit Circus Foundation, our educational nonprofit, we work with schools and remain free to set our own objectives. These include:

- Lowering the barrier of entry in STEAM fields to engage more females and students of color
- Promoting an interest in exploration
- Engaging with the students' personal interests
- Guiding students to appreciate the value of what can be gained from a failure

We often start this process with invention competitions, asking students about their interests and encouraging them to research those interests to identify what is missing or what they could bring to that area to make it more accessible, more dynamic, or more appealing to a student. For example, during the pandemic we asked students to identify issues in their home, community, or school that they could address with their ideas and inventions. Our goal with this inquiry is to engage the students in their interests and open doors to their seeing themselves as inventors and creators—the source of valuable ideas. Nolan even proposes that students be given a voice in how the school is run—including when and how they study—and leaves room for them to explore ideas individually or in groups. In his proposal, student input is encouraged, honored, and celebrated.

Children who are encouraged in their interests more easily embrace the opportunity to learn something new. A child with less self-confidence and an underdeveloped interest in a subject or multiple subjects can be afraid to try something new. This is often because they are afraid to fail and afraid to be found lacking.

We encourage students to understand the valuable information that comes with momentary setbacks and failures, even colossal failures. We need to inspire students to think, to consider, to research their interests, and to see their ideas as valuable contributions toward solutions. This has rarely been successfully accomplished with 30 students in a class all following the same curriculum. It may be a little easier in elementary classes, but it becomes nearly impossible in middle and high school education. This is where Nolan's proposal shines.

Critical thinking and problem-solving skills are in high demand and yet not plentiful in current business settings or in academic communities. Twenty years ago the social-emotional health of the culture was rarely considered. Many of our current educators older than 50 were taught to be teachers in the information-delivery method. Many of them are now asking: What is the appropriate way to teach in a socially and emotionally challenging time like the pandemic?

Teaching critical and creative thinking in the curriculum is crucial. The importance of social-emotional considerations in curriculum was mentioned only occasionally in research prior to the 1980s. Between

1980–90 there were 51 research papers that showed up in a search for social-emotional learning. In 2020 alone that same search found 5,180 research papers covering this crucial topic.

We have an education system that honors those whose skill sets include a high degree of competency in memorizing information; we need to broaden that to include the ability to reason, to communicate that reasoning, and to demonstrate competent problem-solving skills. These should count in the measurement of an effective education. However, they do not appear currently to be considered or measured. In Nolan's vision, these skills are not just honored, they are developed, encouraged, and considered in the evaluation process.

All too often in education today, we measure what students can regurgitate in a test or final exam. We rarely see questions that allow a student to demonstrate their understanding of the material and the way they came to that understanding. This is also true of how we arrange the school day. We honor those who can thrive in a system that is organized around administration and the teachers' desired schedules rather than one that would allow the student to best absorb material. We have research that identifies the best hours to teach elementary students and when best to teach high school students. Yet that information does not have any impact on the school day. The research is convincing and is not in dispute. Yet we keep the school day as it is, in complete disregard for what would be best for the students.

It is on us as educators to develop a system that will nurture social-emotional learning and honor the skills that create competent problem solvers. It is the difference between nurturing a growth mindset over a fixed one. It's important to honor the natural skills of a child, their natural curiosity, and in some cases their interest in research. Perhaps their keen sense of process has them reading about a topic; we can encourage that by engaging them in subject matter they're interested in and then asking them to research that topic. Our goal should be to help them see where their curiosity and skills can take them. Done effectively, this will encourage a growth mindset. It is much easier for a child to learn if they see themselves as evolving and capable. Critical thinking and problem-solving become second nature. These are the skills that the future will demand of them.

We often ask teachers to engage with students in new ways to develop habits that can lead to impactful life skills, but we often ask this without preparing them for how to do it. We need a curriculum that will engage both teachers and students while addressing the need for their development of critical thinking and problem-solving skills.

> Much of the information delivered in education can be buried in a game that seamlessly delivers education and that requires critical thinking and problem-solving skills to acquire trophies and rewards inside the games. Escape rooms are an example of how you can make problem-solving inviting to students.

In January 2020, as CEO of the Two Bit Circus Foundation, I attended the ED Games Expo in Washington, DC. This is where participants are offered hands-on experience with the games funded by the Department of Education during the previous year. Working directly with these games helped solidify my conviction that the current thinking about games is limited and can be superseded with a fundamentally new paradigm. And my conviction that we here at ExoDexa can do better than other educational-product designers is rooted in my direct experience of the products that the Department of Education presented at the Expo.

To be able to see all those products assembled together was an experience of considerable privilege. It gave me an understanding of the state of current practice and the best elements of each of these products. It also informed my desire and passion for this collaboration with Nolan. To work with the father of video games to build out the platforms that could engage students in a deeper and more meaningful way is indeed a step in the right direction. Add to that a complete rethinking of the educational system from the ground up—which is sorely needed—and it's clear that Nolan brings significant value to the conversation.

As educators, creating compelling games was not part of our curriculum-development training. We know what we want to teach and what thoughts we want to provoke. However, we are competing for the students' attention with highly engaging video games. The game industry knows how to keep kids in their games and aspiring to the next level. It is our assertion that this same goal can be accomplished in education with the right parties at the table. It is hard to imagine turning a middle school student into a lifelong learner if we make those first seven or eight years of learning boring, uninteresting, or confusing.

Marshall McLuhan was a media theorist in the 1960s who wrote, among other topics, about education. One of his notable comments was, "All media is educational." Basically, these games are already teaching kids things: They are teaching them that Orcs are on the Horde Faction, Rogues have lockpicking ability, and to unlock level 12, you have to find the secret passage behind the palm tree—and so on and so forth. The games are teaching kids facts, strategies, and even muscle memory.

I find McLuhan's argument stimulating because it shows that we don't need to demonstrate that video games can teach; they already do. All media teaches. The question is, of course, *what* does it teach? Is it valuable to the kids, their future, and society? What we're doing at ExoDexa is putting the right content in the game medium.

TESTS DISGUISED AS GAMES

To gain the attention of the student when we are in competition with all of the exciting, well-designed games they are playing in their free time, we need to create enjoyable distractions. These distractions can also be in the form of games that just happen to deliver education. We need games that promote creative thinking and that hone critical thinking as users progress through the game using creative problem-solving skills. And, in our case, we expect the games to instill a sense of environmental stewardship into these future adults.

These proposed games would require that the player acquire knowledge, or certain skills, to move forward. The game could inspire engagement and, if done well, encourage the student to take agency over their education. Could designers create a game that requires math equations to open levels? One that offers rewards in the game to keep the student engaged as they level up? Why not? We would know what new knowledge is gained by where the student is in the game, eliminating the need for tests. The game, in essence, becomes a test—without looking like a test or causing the anxiety commonly found around testing. Again, games that require problem-solving and creative and critical-thinking skills to beat it will educate without lectures, without traditional testing, and with the student's full engagement.

If you put children with a diagnosis for attention deficit disorder in front of a video game they like, they can stay focused for hours. Also, academic subjects should be taught in 15-minute modules, which is in keeping with current research about attention spans for kids and adults when absorbing new information.

A perfect scenario for the future of education would look like this: Academic experts design engaging curriculum, and game designers serve this content in an engaging game format that encourages students to exhibit grit and perseverance. Students should need curiosity and a growth mindset to beat the game. It is on us as educators to pique the students' interest and nurture the skill set of critical and creative thinking and problem-solving. We will have covered a lot of ground if this collaboration between educators and game designers can be done in this format.

In recent years, many educators have called for the gamification of as much curriculum as possible. Current offerings in educational games emerge from a spectrum of sources, most of them separate from the vibrant and highly interactive world of professionally designed games. As an educator, I see that the current generation of educational games is informed by well-structured lesson planning. Where there is considerable room for growth is in understanding what makes a game deeply compelling, perhaps even addictive. Academics don't consider the "game loop" when designing games. This loop—the ability to draw the player through a set of deeply engaging puzzles of progressive difficulty and to gain commitment from the player—is where the professional gaming industry excels.

In order to see this kind of dynamic change through to a successful completion, we need to involve game designers. Inviting these experts to help us create games that encourage critical thinking would be an effective first step.

I encourage a relationship between education and the game-design community and would go so far as to say there should be generous tax benefits for game companies that develop games for education. (More on that later.) The immediate question is who would we most want involved in this collaboration from the video game world?

Nolan Bushnell, founder of the modern video game.

WHOSE NEEDS SHOULD COME FIRST
IN THE CLASSROOM?

No society can thrive if it throws a significant portion of their citizens under the bus. Today our public school systems are doing just that. Every child who drops out of school without a meaningful set of skills will often end up costing society a substantial price in remediation or incarceration. They are unlikely to ever reach their potential. That price is too high. Efficiency is important in any activity, and those who view profit as a dirty word are probably a product of a failed school system. Without the profit motive, systems become lazy, inefficient, and bloated. The profit motive substitutes for political largesse. For some reason efficiency tends to be left out of the dialogue, as though efficiency is a dirty word as well. It is not. Efficiency is value for money. It provides the basis for continued improvement.

The effective system has to be laser focused on outcomes. We need to create the best-trained, best-educated citizens in the world. Only then can we hope to maintain a high standard of living and our ideal of equal opportunity. We cannot continue to create a permanent underclass of dysfunctional citizens who have little hope and often end up in prison or suffer an early death.

Outcomes depend on merit. Any structure that attempts to substitute another metric is less efficient and sacrifices something. In studying schools for the last 20 years, one cannot

continued

help but come to the conclusion that our current state of public schools is a direct result of creating an educational system based on political squabbles rather than on seeking long-term positive outcomes for students. Students are simply a pawn in a game that use them as a marketing ploy to continue to spend tax money extracted from a populace unwisely and inefficiently.

I am acutely aware of how true Nolan's words are in terms of how school administrators often seem to be working against the best interest of the student. But this is a difficult area to navigate from within the educational system.

A system that puts students' needs ahead of the balance of the constituents, teachers, administrators, and support staff is a system I can get behind. We need a refresh. Teachers need to have the ability to excel when the students excel. Merit pay and metrics that help us rate teachers' effectiveness would be welcome.

Young, energetic teachers receive low pay and minimal pension contributions, even if they teach and coach better than more senior teachers. Over half of new teachers quit teaching within five years. There are times when many older, burned-out, dysfunctional teachers—with high seniority—are massively overpaid. When a bad teacher has little or no accountability for outcomes, the classroom becomes a death sentence for the kids. The kids then have to endure or vote with their feet and leave school.

In consideration of the issues we face in education and in light of what Nolan describes in terms of rewards, I am open to considering his plan for rewarding both educators and students. There is plenty in this book to challenge your (and my) ideas about education.

I learned from Chuck E. Cheese that when it comes to kids, the laser focus has to be on them and not on anyone else. I am a father of eight children and was quick to seek a different school if I felt my kids' needs were not being met. I was lucky because I had the means to give my family that flexibility. My older daughters went to public elementary school but attended boarding school in Hawaii for junior and senior high. All the rest of my children went to public elementary and junior high in the Portola Valley school system and then to private high schools. I realize now that Portola Valley public schools had little in common with a real public school. The area was rich, and all the parents were quite involved.

I remember several teachers who were drummed out of the school system. My wife would even sit in the classes of prospective teachers. If there were several teachers teaching that grade the following year, she would demand that our kids got the teacher that she deemed to be the best. She is someone who cannot be denied. We had clout. We held several fundraisers for the school at our home; one raised almost a quarter of a million dollars. That is a far cry from what most experience in public schools. I want everyone to have the ability to get as good an education as my kids. It is doable.

I relate to Nolan's concern that some are getting a great education and others are being left behind. My daughter teaches at a private school, and my grandchildren go with her every day. I am a believer in public education and feel some guilt over the difference that my grandchildren experience in their school. The difference is significant. The training the teachers receive, the engagement of the parents, the expectations the teachers have for the children regarding their engagement, and their responsibility to their studies is so different from what is being offered in the public school system, except perhaps in a few high-functioning schools with extraordinary principals and support staff working with motivated teachers. It isn't just the money involved, it is the entire system that serves the students better than the current public system. The parents of the public school students would often love to be involved but have to work too many hours to truly contribute. On top of that, public school isn't always a welcoming environment for parents.

> We can fix this. All we have to do is measure everything and let no one hide in bureaucracy or the classroom. Truth and light will allow for good decisions.
>
> Not only can we fix this system—I believe we can do it within five years. These fixes will come in a variety of ways.

There is nothing like a deadline to motivate action. Given what I know about Nolan's system and ExoDexa's ability to track the full learning experience, there is hope that in five years we could address the main issues outlined in this book. Of course, implementing it in the public school system will be a challenge. In my experience, education moves more slowly than nearly any other governmental department. My confidence lies in the fact that we have an opportunity to implement more quickly than might be true in the public school system. The key will be in data collection and distribution of the findings.

We need to spend resources wisely, and if we do, the economy should be able to sustain GDP growth rates at the 5 percent to 8 percent level. The current two-tier education system in which rich kids enjoy good schools using current proven effective methods while poor kids get standards established decades ago is the pathway to a permanent underclass and a future class war. Not every student needs to go to college. Nor should every job require a college education.

In normal times, the economy naturally grows to the point that inflation causes the Federal Reserve to tighten interest rates. We will approach this dynamic in the years to come. The problem is that employee inflation always comes from a paucity of talent. The skilled get bid up in price, while there is still large unemployment of the unskilled. If we increase the supply of skilled workers, the economy can grow faster without igniting inflation. Without a good educational system, the educated rich get richer and the uneducated poor get poorer. That's not a good situation.

As I said, we can fix this. We can again lead the world in innovation and show the world how to fix education. Everyone will thank us.

EXPANDING OUR REACH

I am a big fan of Nolan's optimism on this subject. I agree that this is a manageable problem. The road block has been the system's resistance to change. Coming from the outside and developing a system that can be tested in schools in need of change offers the ability to build success in the real world. Once we are past the testing stage, with data collected over several years and beyond our initial test groups, we can offer our programs at both the state and federal level, as we will have deeper data to back up our claims. I am confident that, done well, this system of educating students has international potential.

This isn't just an American problem, and we are currently working with school systems around the world to address the need for change. Educators everywhere are concerned about students' abilities to think critically and solve problems. They worry that children often won't start something if they don't already know how to do it or at least have step-by-step instruction. The world needs problem solvers, and education to date has not been great at building that muscle.

I am not a formal educator but a scientist who believes that all problems are soluble and that new systems can be designed through crowdsourcing that taps the collective wisdom of the world. All of us are smarter than any one of us.

ExoDexa will provide the arena by breaking down the syllabus into nano-learning chunks and providing the assessment, not as tests but hidden in games. That will enable educators with few technical skills to use and curate highly interactive curriculums that use the guiding principles of adaptive practice. Providing there's a market outlet, many highly skilled programmers will choose to augment these tools for even better outcomes. The world then will provide the solutions, and the fastest way to teach a concept to a random selection of kids will win. This structure will bring the creativity of millions to this project and reward them. This will be just the first step, because learning is more complex than simply speed in learning a concept. Testing retention is another valuable attribute that can be added in games, relieving the stress students experience when they know they are being tested.

Other areas of refinement needed in education include determining what combination of learning styles each student prefers. We know that there are countless different ways that optimize individual outcomes.

There are also differences in kids' cultural backgrounds and different home situations that will impact when and how students are best positioned to learn.

The ExoDexa system will measure everything. The data will be open source and anonymized. The world will be free to find correlations and propose tests, curriculum, methodology. The ideas that work will bubble to the top. The issues are massive. We have kids with wildly different backgrounds and starting points. There are kids with varying innate capabilities, kids with great parents, no parents, and bad parents. Here in the United States, there are kids who have been here all their life

continued

and kids who just arrived and do not speak a word of English. We have abused kids and psychologically damaged kids. Add to those factors changes of puberty and all the strangeness that the new flood of hormones cause in kids at just the time they are starting to figure out what is going on.

People in academia want to have real-time research and a system agile enough to adjust and self-correct. Currently, changes in the national approach to educating our kids can take decades. Often by the time the change is made there is a need for new changes. Real-time adjustments measured in real time is the way of the future.

The previous litany of differences is just the start. Some kids are better in the morning and others function better later. All are seeking either engagement or escape. Most are worried about the future and how they will fit in. Other kids do not believe they have a future. There are so many questions and so little help. Thirty-five kids in a class means that few out-of-the-norm questions are answered—yet all the kids are out of the norm in one way or another.

In short, classrooms do not work. There is just not enough resonance, except for the cookie-cutter kid. And the cookie cutter cuts off part of every kid to whom it is applied. Those who conform to the cookie cutter often leave behind their creativity, which is the worst of amputations.

CULTIVATE CREATIVITY

The late Sir Ken Robinson wrestled with this subject in 2006 during his first TED Talk called "Do Schools Kill Creativity?" He made it clear that he believed the system of education applied in industrial nations stomps the creativity out of children. He urged us to make changes to protect children from this reality. He claimed that creativity is as important as literacy and that we should treat it as such. It was clear from the outburst of applause from his audience and the 70 million viewers who have seen this TED Talk that he was not alone in claiming that schools are stripping our children of their natural creativity.

He went beyond saying that we should merely *include* the arts; he noted that the arts should be given the same weight and attention as science, technology, engineering, and math, the STEM disciplines. This is actually how I originally bonded with Brent Bushnell, Nolan's eldest son, who is the chairman of the board of the Two Bit Circus Foundation for which I am CEO. We were both working in Los Angeles and were the two most vocal supporters of STEAM over STEM.

Classrooms today are one size and one speed fits all. There are many things that are sacrificed once one chooses a classroom with the teacher in front and kids sitting and watching. In this tyranny of the classroom, kids have to start at the same time, and there has to be a group that arrives at the same time to settle down and be quiet. They have to pay attention, and if they don't understand something, the process stops, while the kids that do get it are bored.

Students who do not understand do not speak up and are just lost. How are the kids graded? Tests and/or homework is the norm. No one asks if the students have mastery. Do they

continued

cheat? Is there bias in paper corrections? Are there kids who are left in confusion? The system is too generalized in the way the children are batch processed. There needs to be a finer grained and more nuanced approach.

Teachers should not teach in a classroom. The one-to-many delivery methods are wrong and no longer work. They have never worked well, but 30 years ago there were few alternatives. In years past, school was the most interesting thing happening in town; the alternative was watching the river flow and the corn grow.

Tom Sawyer and Huckleberry Finn did not like school much, because outside they saw a rich, dynamic world without structure. Today kids see an outside world rich in technology and communications tools compared to their schools, which tend to be lacking in technology and the newest communication models.

Yet, we *can* make school fun. We can find out what engages students, and we can teach skills that fit the world of today and that will also provide students with multiple ways of making an extraordinary living. We can remediate some of the damage their circumstances have caused and give students access to the steps they need to get out of poverty or despair.

What if the dynamic of sitting still and listening is wrong? The image of a kid with rapt attention absorbing knowledge is seldom achieved. The only time I see kids exhibiting focused attention is when they are actively solving problems they encounter in video games.

Imagine students in an environment with physical movement and rapt attention while learning and actively solving problems, building things, learning strategies, learning musical instruments, dancing, and making movies for YouTube. What if they were also operating a business on eBay? Imagine learning physics or chemistry while playing a video game.

A GLOBAL ECONOMY AND INTERNATIONAL FRIENDSHIPS

The fact is that the most successful entrepreneurs in the world did not finish college. In the next 20 years could it be that the most successful people will not finish high school? No one knows what the next 20 years will be like, only that it will be quite different from what is happening now. There are no safe paths to security or riches. In the global economy, the college degree becomes a commodity that could actually cheapen the economic value of the holder. Many will never see a return on the debt they take on for a degree that does not matter in the workforce.

The Chinese will graduate more college graduates than the rest of the world combined. They beat most of the rest of the world in STEM subjects. I would, however, prefer hiring a kid who has dropped out of high school in California and has taught herself programming as a hobby to pursue video

continued

games than an engineer from China with a master's degree. Why? Because the high school kid is driven by a passion for creative problem-solving, and the Chinese master's student is more likely to be driven by the status symbol of the degree. And the process of getting that degree likely drained all their potential creativity.

Our high school dropout was able to avoid that state by becoming passionate about games and technology and in some ways was inoculated from the attempts of our school system to push her into a box. We know that creativity drops as a student becomes educated. If creativity is the dominant, most important factor 20 years from now, perhaps we should all have fourth graders on our advisory boards.

It will be interesting to see which countries adopt the ExoDexa model. If our projected outcomes are true or even close, the adoption should be rapid. Since schools can form an interesting network of students and teachers, it is likely that social studies and world government courses will become globally interactive and personal. Language training will become relevant, and students can become citizens of the world by expanding their horizons, knowledge, and empathy. It has always been a reality that putting knowledge in context and practice makes learning "stickier" and more relevant.

As modules become multilingual, a larger number of learning methods will be tested. A math module for the Chinese should differ only slightly from those of the English-speaking countries. It may be that there is a particular way that different

language use causes different approaches that may be reso-
nant with a section of students in other countries. Reading the
writings of Camus in French is said to be much more rewarding
than the translations into English.

Learning about different tax laws and government systems can bring into contrast our own government principles
and perhaps show ways the United States and other countries
could improve outcomes. Supporting entrepreneurship in the
schools would be impossible in certain countries that severely
limit and restrict company formation or cause such liability for
the founders that no one does it. Often the stark contrast and
kids' awareness may do much to cut the bureaucracy in these
difficult countries.

It is true that some countries score higher on international measurement tools regarding academics, but not all of them have been
able to support childhood mental health inside that measurement.
Students in Japan have some of the highest suicide rates among teens.
According to the newspaper *This Week in Asia*, the overall rate of suicide has dropped steadily over the last decade except with teens, and a
report by Sammy Heung[1] claims that academic pressure from parents
is often the stated reason. The need to make education more relevant
to the individual child and more engaging for the student isn't just a
good idea, it is essential.

---

1 Sammy Heung, "Suicide the Cause in Nearly a Quarter of Hong Kong Child Deaths Reviewed by
Coroner's Court," *South China Morning Post*, November 23, 2021, https://www.scmp.com/news/hong-kong/
health-environment/article/3157126/suicide-cause-nearly-quarter-hong-kong-child.

We will recruit some of the best mathematicians, biologists, physicists, and specialists in as many fields as the students need. With an online service, the ability to aggregate the students who desire this level of coaching makes this possible. Often someone with these skills can be accessed internationally; they can take a second job because of the time differences. A scientist working at a lab in Europe can help an American student because off-hours in Europe coincide with the student's regular class time. Also, because of the differences in cost of living, a modest payment to a curator of antiquities in Egypt, for example, will make tutoring American kids attractive.

Many people in business or politics would love to help passionate kids. A video link makes this service a simple way to make our schools really hum. In the same way that an Uber driver can choose when to work and when to clock out, a tutor or mentor can work when they have the time and take off when they don't. These people can do more than tutor math or physics, they can talk about what it is like in industry and what it is like to work at Apple or Intel. This contact with capable people can often be more important than the actual subject mentoring.

Foreign-language subjects are a natural for long-distance teaching, training, and practice. Linking students with other students and teachers abroad who are native to the culture and the language would provide a superior experience over a native English-speaking teacher teaching German. Developing relationships with students in other countries will go beyond learning a language to help the student understand the culture that accompanies a language.

Maya Angelou, when talking about our level of understanding and acceptance of others, said that there isn't a person we couldn't forgive if we heard their full story. Exposing students to other cultures at a young age and helping them establish friendships around the world will help us heal generations of hatred between cultures. Every new life born into a culture represents the potential to establish new realities and build on stories of inclusion and acceptance.

MEETING SOCIAL NEEDS OF STUDENTS

Kids who are slow to learn can benefit the most from the ExoDexa system. It is often difficult to find out exactly what the problem is with an individual student. Many children don't start reading early on in life. Their parents may have been working multiple jobs. There may have been siblings to care for a newborn arriving. There may have been no one reading to the child or anyone reading in the house that the child would see and copy. When a child doesn't learn to read well by third grade, the problem is compounded as they move up in school. The first few grade levels are about teaching a child to read; from third grade forward it is reading to learn.

Students may have social problems. If a damaging home life is the issue, that child needs a different kind of experience than the child struggling with reading. It could well be that both learning to read and social issues are problems for a student. In that case, until the underlying problems are addressed, academic goals will be harder to reach. However, software can

continued

help identify and support a student. We can also constantly be conducting invisible testing in an attempt to understand the types of problems each child is addressing in their life. Once we understand the issue, we can offer support and assignments that focus on the unique type of cognitive difficulty the student presents.

Some students require a little more contact than others. Once we know that about a student, in theory we can organize academic mentors. The problem in our current system is that we don't have the tools to identify the problem nor the time for the teacher to address it in the classroom setting.

Some students gather up their assignments and head out to accomplish their tasks. Others struggle to get organized and waste a good deal of time before they actually get started tackling the issues. These students need help. Sometimes they just need a sounding board, preferably one who understands kids, education, and scaffolding ideas with students. Others need more hand-holding until they find their passion. Really, who better than a teacher to do that? The challenge is freeing up the teachers' time so they can address these needs without neglecting or holding back others who are ready to head to the next task.

There are excellent teachers with many years of experience who would volunteer to be a sounding board for a student.

Other students may need more directed mentoring. In that case we would hire a mentor on a schedule. Many retired and active teachers would love to work a few hours a week for personal reward and augmented retirement income.

It is my belief that all students are exceptional students. It is our job to help them unwrap and nurture their exceptionalness. It often takes a respected voice in a child's life to point out the characteristics that make that child unique and talented in a particular area, and then for that voice or other respected voices in that child's world to help the child nurture their talent, become self-directed in building on that talent, and make the most of that talent.

Exceptional students range from bright to slow, but there are also exceptional students who are emotionally fragile and going through difficult life challenges. In today's schools there is no easy way to quickly get help to a student for certain types of problems. The ExoDexa mentor/tutoring network allows for experts who can counsel a student who is concerned about whatever issues are presenting. This is the time in life when young people need to have trusted adults in their community so they can talk about difficult subjects and seek advice when needed.

Some mentors/tutors will be known to the student in the same way a digital classroom teacher isn't exactly like the in-classroom teacher but is known to the student. In other instances, the student will be working with an anonymous

continued

mentor/tutor. They may be anonymous to the student but not to the ExoDexa system; this person has been LiveScanned and trained in the approach and philosophy of our system. An anonymous link becomes an important lifeline to some students.

CHAPTER 2

Our Primary Goals

Nolan proposes that education fit into realities that are similar to business. There are processes in place that help organizations meet their market's needs and follow certain patterns in order to do so effectively enough to make the business profitable and in demand.

Every success system has four parts:

1. Goals

2. Strategy

3. Tactics

4. Measurements

If the strategy and tactics are correct, the goals are achievable and can be measured.

GOALS FOR THE SCHOOL OF THE FUTURE

- Make school fun for a lifelong love of learning, curiosity, and progress.

- Give students the skills to be productive members of society.

- Instill healthy habits in nutrition and exercise.

- Impart business skills and entrepreneurship.

- Teach creative problem-solving skills.

- Have a school day free from boredom.

- Instill optimism and enthusiasm.

- Find hidden talents in each student.

Nolan's experience with success adds significant weight to his assertions. Education and business share a desire to get it right and to be able to prove their research with hard data. For education, we know what the goals are for each grade level, we have strategies and tactics in place to attempt to reach those goals, and we use test scores to measure our success. Few would consider the results to indicate consistent success, however, and that is what we are working on here.

In the case of education, there are children's minds on the line, and getting it right is imperative—especially following 2020/21, two years during which most students lost the equivalent of between 57 and 230-plus days of classroom learning (according to statistics from the US Department of Education that was shared with us on a call on January 14, 2021). Those numbers are both disturbing and depressing. We will need radical interventions to make up for this year. Yet it will be hard for business-as-usual folks to help with the change needed. We need outside voices involved in the planning and goal setting to deal with this crisis.

The ability to fast-track research in Nolan's program and address concerns in real time is exciting. We need to be able to share the story of how we got it right or wrong using data. Another goal of the education community is to make the findings available for peer review and, ultimately, to share the findings that will enable other progressive educators, schools, and districts to evaluate those findings and apply what works in their environment. In this format there is room for teacher training to support other educational ecosystems and influence the more conservative community with data-confirming effective methods.

We have new iPhones every year and new car designs yearly, and yet education has not changed in any significant way for decades, some might say for the full hundred-plus years of public education. The ability to guide this change will require data derived from measurement tools other than test scores. Nolan presents a compelling case in the chapters ahead for testing that is hidden in game format.

MEASURE THE ABILITY
TO THINK, NOT MEMORIZE

We need an effective way to inspire students to push themselves academically. When it comes to creating a desire to learn and the ability to establish habits of lifelong learning, we need help. Some students see education as a way to move into a new way of life. They prepare for testing in which we challenge them on their ability to retain information. What we really need to measure, however, is their ability to think, plan, adjust, solve problems, and/or deal with stress. These are all skills that will be valued far beyond the years of formal education.

These skills are not something you can google for an answer the way you can the facts and figures of past education practices. We need more time in school that nurtures these skills and traits and measures the student's ability to think their way through a problem or situation. We need programs that address social and emotional learning and the development of the whole student. These are topics being discussed in education, and being tested in a few innovative schools. These are the opportunities we are tasked with engaging in and the problems we need to resolve.

Education the way we are accustomed to delivering it is not possible for the foreseeable future because of the pandemic's impact, which has lasted longer than any of those in charge are willing to accept, or, if they do accept it, they are reluctant to admit. Let me restate the obvious: As we return to the classroom, if we go back to business as usual in education, we will have missed a significant opportunity.

This is our chance to rethink our approach to educating the next generation. Nolan has created a blueprint, and in the next few chapters we will examine that plan.

Many students lost crucial classroom time during the pandemic. Teachers had a hard time getting the kids to log on and do their classwork, and there were many conversations about how to compel students to log on and what the consequences should be for not logging into class. USC had Arnold Schwarzenegger on a panel about education, and he suggested that we needed to do something to make up for this lost time. He offered a few ideas that centered around adding time, a day or a few hours a day. I believe we have a greater impact by changing what we offer the students rather than how much time we need them in our classrooms.

Nolan is proposing a system designed to make logging on compelling for students. He outlines what we can do to make the process enjoyable and engaging. These are productive conversations for in-person as well as distance learning. As schools reopen, we need a plan that can make up for the lost time and build bridges to new learning systems that captivate the child and motivate them to take agency over their education. The plan Nolan outlines goes a long way toward that goal.

This ambition for education is what made the idea of working with Nolan to plan and design the school of the future so exciting. His plan is directly in line with what I see as lacking in the education system to date. I've heard Nolan talk about engaging kids in self-directed exploration, and his ideas are inspirational.

I'd like to look at what Nolan considers to be the platform for success in ventures from the perspective of the academic community and the current thinking about goals in particular.

IDENTIFYING GOALS

A couple of academic researchers, Dale Schunk and Barry Zimmerman, have focused on research exploring the impact of motivation on self-directed learning. As part of their study, they published a collection of research papers in *Motivation and Self-Regulated Learning*.[2] Their goal was to better understand the role motivation plays in a student's ability to self-regulate. I know, it doesn't exactly sound like a must read from the title, but in our case, it is imperative.

There was a great deal written by these two regarding the importance of goals—in particular, goals that are set and negotiated by the individual committing to the goals. They also include the research conducted by respected scholars collaborating on the findings that motivation is key to self-regulation as a learner. In this case we are talking about the goals the school shares with parents and educators. But the findings also pertain to students negotiating their own goals and building that internal argument while they share and debate with contemporaries.

Schunk and Zimmerman also emphasized the importance of sharing and brainstorming those goals with peers. This has proven an effective approach and is borne out of the deep dive into that existing

2   D. H. Schunk, B. J. Zimmerman, eds., *Motivation and Self-Regulated Learning: Theory, Research, and Applications* (Taylor & Francis Group, 2008).

research about goal setting and self-regulated learning by Schunk and Zimmerman that resulted in the publishing of the studies. And these are not only from their own research but confirmed by numerous and widespread research teams. The value of this collaboration of researchers is that they either confirm or disprove theories, and in this incidence confirming the theory as they came to similar conclusions.

Being motivated to reach their goals can also inform grit and determination in a student. These are skills that are more obvious in students who are required to find work-arounds in their education. Sometimes this is necessitated by a learning challenge and other times because of home-life realities. When things don't come easily, you find work-arounds if you are motivated. This is not as easily developed in students of privilege. The ability to solve problems quickly because there are finances to disperse doesn't easily inform grit and determination in the child. These skills, developed at a young age, inform the future coping skills of the child as an adult.

RELYING ON MENTORS TO HELP

Usually (especially when you are young) you talk an idea and goals through a few times before you write them out. Every time a child shares their ideas and goals, they bring a larger community into the process. Sharing your thoughts with friends and mentors helps to refine your goals and cement them. There is some wisdom in the premise that we don't know what we think until we write about it. The bottom line is that research backs Nolan on this. If the strategy and tactics are correct, the goals are achievable and measurable and the impact on the student is invaluable.

According to the research on motivation and self-directed learning, when students are engaged in the setting of goals, it encourages a personal commitment to reaching the goals and a strong sense of agency over their education. Moreover, the student who has been engaged in negotiating and setting their goals is more likely to have shared their thoughts and interests with their mentors.

Nolan's vision for ExoDexa relies on understanding students' interests to promote engagement and helping them claim their education.

INSPIRE CURIOSITY AND
A LIFELONG LOVE OF LEARNING

Students currently show up to school because they have to or because they have meals there with their friends. Some lucky students have teachers they like and interests they can pursue. Seldom do they show up because they are so engaged in their education that they can't wait to get back to whatever project they are working on. That needs to change.

Mitchel Resnick, the author of *Lifelong Kindergarten* and a 30-plus-year veteran of the MIT Media Lab, writes extensively about the importance of creative space in education. He outlines what he calls the Creative Learning Spiral as a cycle formed from imagining, creating, playing, sharing, reflecting, and reimagining. In his opinion there has been a strong negative impact from the loss of creative time at school over the past couple of decades. Resnick writes, "Unfortunately, after kindergarten, most schools shift away from the Creative Learning Spiral . . . too often, schools focus on delivering instruction and information rather than supporting students in the creative learning process."[3] In doing this, schools miss the opportunity to develop problem-solving skills.

Educators are constantly seeking ways to engage students. In this effort they attend professional-development events, search online

3   Mitchel Resnick, *Lifelong Kindergarten: Cultivating Creativity through Projects, Passion, Peers, and Play* (Cambridge: The MIT Press, 2018), p. 13.

resources, and share success stories of best practices with each other. I'm aware of this and celebrate the reality of teachers' commitment. Most teachers are motivated by the potential of a positive impact on a student. But these teachers are limited in the impact they can have, because of class sizes especially. The pandemic and half-baked virtual tools given to teachers haven't helped either.

Nolan is proposing that we harness well-designed technology to help students engage in their education. Technology allows us to personalize the learning experience for each student based on their interests, their level of competency, and their ability to apply themselves to their interests. These are far more important goals than finding a class schedule that works for all 30–35 children.

CULTIVATING EVERY CHILD'S INTERESTS

Curiosity is the first requirement for our educators. It is a doorway to all pursuits. Curiosity promotes exploration, which leads to learning, and then it becomes like the song that never ends. Satisfying curiosity often inspires the next level of exploration. Psychologist Jean Piaget claimed that mathematics can be easily taught to any child if you find the interest of the child and create examples that incorporate those interests. This point can't be overstated. We now have the technical ability to do this.

We have known for more than 50 years that children learn differently at different times in their lives and with different methods of engagement—some auditory, some kinesthetic—and yet that concept is rarely applied to the planning of curriculum or in the design of delivery systems.

Most teachers would love to be able to offer an individualized learning program, but the sheer number of students to prepare for makes it impossible. Teachers are already doing lots of work unpaid in their off hours; we cannot expect more. That is completely understandable yet not in the best interest of the students. We need to support teachers and augment their work with technology that can adapt to each learner without placing an undue burden on the teacher. If we are engaging students inside their interests and at their competency level, their commitment will be stronger. And a student who is enjoying the learning process because it is based in their area of interest will be more likely to develop curiosity and a desire for learning that can last a lifetime.

It is disheartening to see children and/or adults who lack curiosity. Small children are curious by nature. They watch, they study, they touch. If the child's basic needs are met—food, a dry diaper, and a cuddle—the baby focuses the rest of their energy on exploring their surroundings. That's pure curiosity. It is the infant's version of what Abraham Maslow called the hierarchy of needs.

If the basic needs are not met, or if a child is mistreated, these issues and experiences can strip a child of natural curiosity and so much more that can linger for a lifetime.

Many believe that school as usual does little to enhance natural curiosity and that the punitive educational system is partly responsible for reducing creativity in children. Our goal in education should include making room for teachers and students to follow an idea as far as they are inspired to take the search.

OUR PROJECT-BASED LEARNING RESULTS

In 2013 I attended an event at the California Science Center that was a fundraiser for the Partnership for Los Angeles Schools. Some of the teachers we had worked with were there with students who were displaying their senior-year projects made with our materials and supervised by teachers we had trained in project-based learning. One of the students had a model home she had built for a project we call Light It Up. The students are challenged to build a model home and, using one battery, install three separate switches to run from that battery. In this way we are checking off several points in the science curriculum, but that isn't how it is presented to the students.

The students have a challenge—three switches, one battery, make it work. One senior had created a beautiful model home with curtains on the windows, floor covering, and she even had magnets on the refrigerator. It was a full-on art project for her. When I asked her about her plans for the future, she told me she was heading to Berkeley on a scholarship to study engineering. When I asked how she became interested in engineering, she told me her teacher helped her to see the artistic need in architecture and engineering. She had never seen herself as someone with talent or even interest in the STEM subjects. It was her art that led her to the STEM disciplines. She was the first in her family to finish high school and now would be the first to attend university.

There will be much more in this book about the value of including the A (for Arts) in STEAM education, but the point here is that it is a gateway to students' engagement. It is the candy, the reward, and the motivation for many students.

It is imperative that we meet people where they are and help them establish goals from that point of view. This is true for students, teaching staff, and parents. There are students who need to be active and moving to think—that may mean a walk in the neighborhood, a bike ride, a need to dance. I remember coming home from first grade (there was no kindergarten in rural Canada) and telling my mother that I wasn't going back. My argument in favor of my declaration was that we sat at a desk all day. I was a kid growing up on a farm. I spent my days with animals, in the fields, and in the creeks. There was little time for sitting still. This argument made perfect sense to me, although my mother did convince me to give it another try. I never loved school, but there were other kids there, so I agreed to stay.

If we want kids to have a lifelong love of learning, it would benefit us to make learning enjoyable. If we added regular and rigorous movement, perhaps some bug watching and building of birdhouses (or anything they are interested in building) to the curriculum, we might engage the students on a deeper level and have them motivated to come back.

"BEATS BY ME":
MIDDLE SCHOOLERS MAKE HEADSETS

For the last six years we have offered a summer camp for mostly middle school kids. The first year we had the students, who were 8 to 12 years old, make working headsets. We call this project Beats by Me. There was some pushback since this is usually an AP physics project, but everyone agreed to keep it as an option and give it a try.

All the kids chose this option. We asked the kids to make a design and label it (language arts), make it for a particular budget (there were mock prices on everything, adding math to the learning), and make a presentation (writing and reporting) for their parents on the final day. The presentation outlines the benefits of their headset and why they believe it should be manufactured and available to purchase.

At the end of the two weeks, all of the campers had a working headset. Some of the campers failed to get sound a dozen times; other campers stepped up and helped. When students had finished their own headset, they worked with campers who were struggling. We didn't make anything or fix anyone's creation; we simply gave the kids space and encouraged them to help each other. When I was a kid in school, that was called cheating. Now we need students to know how to collaborate. Collaboration is key. When you read success stories, you rarely hear someone saying they did it all themselves. Knowing how to engage with each other is essential.

At the end of camp we interviewed each of the campers about the experience of making their headset. It was clear from their descriptions that learning took place as a result of the experience, punctuated by the need to think the project through and write about it. The kids documented the mistakes made while building the mechanism. They examined what it was that brought sound. In doing this they developed a stronger understanding of how sound is transmitted. These campers could explain the process almost as well as the physics teacher we interviewed—and we have the video to prove the success.

Nearly everyone has a story about their experience in elementary and or middle school. It is either a story about how the system worked for them and why, or how it failed them and the reason. Some kids like order and quiet; those kids did well in the system. But some need noise and movement. Many of us were in the noise and movement group, but few teachers were happy with that track. I like that Nolan points to the importance of building movement into the curriculum. Not only is it important, it offers those kids who need movement an option for their mode of learning.

Encouraging a lifelong love of learning could be propelled by knowing the student, by understanding their interests, and by putting opportunities in front of them that align with their interests. It is also easier to move a student into new areas of interest when they see where their interest intersects with another. That is one way we attempt to build the intellectual muscle, an intense relationship with curiosity with a corresponding thought process, and a growth mindset that this generation of students will need to thrive.

VIDEO GAMES HELP STUDENTS SET GOALS

If we create compelling video games to deliver education, we would be engaging the students where most of them are on a daily basis. The child in this scenario would be offered a learning experience in their most comfortable mode of operation—a game. Once they are engaged in and committed to the game, they are more likely to fully immerse themselves in the material they need to understand to unlock the treasures of the game. Most children can quickly and easily tell you what their goal is in the game they are currently playing. It is on us to help them identify the goals in their education.

If students are engaged in identifying goals, our children have a chance at maintaining and building on the curiosity and engagement that comes with a desire to learn. Even that phrase "desire to learn" is a bit misleading. I don't think we get kids to a point where they are, with great enthusiasm, learning for the sake of learning. It is on us to help the child find their interests or pathways to their interest, if those are already identified, and then help them see and own their talents. It is also on us to supply them with support when things don't go well, so they build appropriate coping skills and so that learning is a pleasant experience.

Helping the child adapt to a lifelong love of learning requires helping them experience the excitement they feel when they learn something new about a favorite subject. It is also important for the student to explore other interests that share or contradict their first interest. Once they experience this exposure, they stand a chance to broaden their horizon and challenge preconceived ideas about their other interests. Or they may confirm their belief. In order to influence a child's desire to learn, we need to offer them the opportunity to explore their current interests. When a student uncovers something that helps them realize they could play a part in their favorite sport—or industry, or business, or any experience they love—they are motivated to gain more knowledge. A desire to learn is a natural reaction to curiosity, and curiosity is inspired by an interest.

We are building a curriculum around the desired end result, which is to nurture curious minds and equip those minds with skill sets that will serve them in a career. We are building a culture of respect and requiring kindness among the student body. We will require the same commitment from teachers and support staff. All schools should build this into the core of their educational culture. We are making it a priority. There are few times in an individual's life when we have as much influence as we do when they are young and in school. Inspiring a lifelong love of learning will make childhood engaging and the rest of life more interesting and productive.

In Sir Ken's TED Talk mentioned earlier, about schools killing creativity, he tells the story of a young girl whose name is Gillian Lynne.[4] She inspired his comment about making the arts as important as academics. Gillian was criticized by every teacher for being fidgety and disruptive in elementary school. She was always moving about the room or moving around in her seat. Her mother, at her wit's end, was preparing to request help from a doctor.

In a moment of inspiration, an educator realized that this child needed to move in order to think. This educator told Gillian's mother that the girl wasn't sick or troubled; she didn't need a doctor. Gillian was a child who needed to move to learn. She wasn't being disruptive, she was simply being herself. He went on to suggest that the mother put Gillian in dance classes rather than medicate her.

Another parent might have put her on medication and disciplined her into submission. Instead, Gillian's mother put her in dance classes, where she excelled. It was the introduction to a world in which she could be a success. Gillian became the choreographer for Andrew Lloyd Webber and has created enormous wealth for herself as a result of her need to move to think.

How many children like this have been told to "sit down and learn"? When Gillian was a child, there was no diagnosis called ADHD. Students like her were simply considered bad. After she had spent a painful decade in elementary school, an educator who cared and had the intelligence to question standard practice—an adult who remained curious—saw what this student needed and addressed it. This is also an effective example of something we will drill down on later, when we talk about finding a student's hidden talent.

Nolan has identified this need for movement as part of the approach for his school. There are so many students who will excel as a result of this minor but important addition to the school day and setting.

---

4 Sir Ken Robinson, "Do Schools Kill Creativity," Ted.com, February 2006, https://www.ted.com/talks/sir_ken_robinson_do_schools_kill_creativity.

Research into students' areas of interest will either deepen their interest or cause them to move on to the next. In both cases we are creating a path to a lifelong love of learning while expanding interests and developing a habit of exploring those interests. And we will have offered educators an environment in which they can flourish as educators. As a result, their students acquire the habits of a curious, engaged person. And the cycle continues.

CHAPTER 3

Lifelong Interest Comes with Curiosity

When we engage the student in areas of their own interest, we stand a stronger chance of nurturing a curious mindset that will endure well past their school years. In addition, when we teach entrepreneurship, the business a student establishes during these formative years will inform their future business endeavors; whether their particular business survives the years of education isn't as important as the life lessons gained from the effort.

Malcolm Gladwell, in *Outliers*, talks about the threshold of hours that makes a person an expert in their field. He shares his research and the research of others that indicate 10,000 hours is what's needed to put you at the top of your profession or sport. Why not make what the child does in school count toward those 10,000 hours? What if we made everything kids study in school relevant to their life and their interests?

If the child is interested in cars, encourage that child to explore the history of cars. Who invented the motor, why, what was the motivation? Who collects and restores cars? Who was the first competitor, and where did they get their start? What was the evolution of the car industry? What would you predict for the future of the automotive industry? What ideas do kids have for a product or service that could address any issue or need that they see in the industry? Our job is to encourage questions and motivate the student to do the research to gain a better understanding of all the moving parts of their interest. In this case, the questions all pertain to cars, and any business they might want to establish could be born of this interest.

For other children, fill in the blank on the interest. The questions don't change, only the subject of the inquiry. Current technology offers software programs to give instant feedback on some elements (spelling and grammar), and evolving programs can help with content and evaluation of written work.

The subject of a student's interest isn't as important as the process of finding that interest. Asking the students questions about their interests keeps them engaged. Who is their role model in whatever industry they're interested in? Who was in political office at that time their role model lived or was successful or invented their widget? Is it pre or post whatever event you want them to look into?

Individualized studies require engaging the student in something they are already interested in and asking them questions about that subject, questions that help them see the connectedness of the world and their interest and that help them explore entrepreneurial possibilities that exist. This often inspires new interests and, as a result of the process, they repeat the research on this new topic and absorb the ability to do effective research. Whatever their long-term goals, regardless of future business endeavors, the need to understand research will always be present.

THE IMPORTANCE OF LISTENING

If we want *students* to engage, *we* need to engage. We educators need to listen to their ideas. It's important that we don't evaluate their interests.

That evaluation will be done by them when they do their research and establish their own measurement of its value. We need to truly hear what students have to say about their ambitions and interests. If they don't know where to start or what their interests are, we need to engage in the exploration with them or partner them with a student who is ready to start their venture. While the struggling student develops their personal passion, they will be learning the process through someone else's discoveries.

Some children are growing up in environments without encouragement of any sort that would help them know their interests. Partnering them with a student who is motivated can inspire passion and help build confidence. Since one of the tenets of our approach is kindness, it is a given that the engaged student will be generous with their input and explanations and will have ample opportunities to praise the students they are assisting. Any corrective feedback would be delivered by educators, while positive input will be delivered directly from student to student. In this system the students enhance their own self-esteem and develop as mentors themselves.

There is an illustrated children's book called *The Rabbit Listened*, in which the author, Cori Doerrfeld, hits on an important skill for any parent, educator, or manager—really for any human who interacts with other humans, but for our purposes here, especially children. Don't rush in with solutions. Listen. Let the individual come to their own conclusions, find their own direction and interests. Our job is to support their exploration.

Individualized studies are finally possible because of technology, but they are made effective by educators who embrace the student's ideas as a pathway to discovery. It will sometimes take great patience to wait and listen, but the real learning for the educator and the student is in the listening.

EAT, MOVE, SLEEP

Educators are out there teaching in a difficult situation at the best of times. The 2020–21 school year was anything but the best of times. Teachers had to compete with all the distractions of home during distance learning. Students were dealing with sleep deprivation, depression, and nutritional issues, and these issues continue to be present now that they are back in the classroom. The students' ability to focus is being determined by the depth of these issues. I believe that Nolan's approach could have a positive impact on them and will be a welcome change for most educators.

Having the skills to succeed includes having healthy habits that will help you survive difficult times. The COVID-19 pandemic was a reminder of how important a basic underlying healthy body is and how the world can change too fast for us to catch up if we have years of unhealthy habits. This virus has been extremely difficult for anyone dealing with diabetes, asthma, obesity. Some of the problems are genetic, but many are born of, or at least impacted by, our day-to-day choices. In the ExoDexa system, our goal is to have students understand the concept of food-as-fuel, self-care, and the importance of the rejuvenation that happens while sleeping.

Making sure the students have to move around regularly will help. Offering music they are drawn to for movement and games that require movement without expensive equipment are all part of the plan.

Few would argue with the importance of sound nutrition in a student's life. Exercise is also key to peak performance in any study or eventual career. Nolan's plan to have learners take part in daily physical activities is likely to have a positive impact on student engagement. It could also offer a strong connection to their commitment to completing their learning modules and retention of their studies if the movement is fun and something to look forward to.

LET KIDS MOVE!

Current research suggests that movement can keep depression at bay. Music and movement are a powerful combination for students. Planning a playlist of music they love with positive self-image messages could add to the impact. Tim Griffin of Griffin Ed has been using music to engage students for years. His goal is to put the K–8 curriculum to music. He engages the kids in writing lyrics to popular tunes. Using music kids like with new words that connect to the academic information they are required to learn actually works. Griffin has empirical data to demonstrate the effectiveness of curriculum delivered through music. I have anecdotal observations, thanks to the 7- and 12-year-olds in my family who have been listening to his music since they were toddlers.

If the students choose which activities they engage in, as with academic goal setting, the student is more apt to continue with the activity and commit to the engagement and reap the benefits. Medical research has claimed that sitting is the new smoking for our generation. Can we impress on the next generation the need to move and to keep their bodies fit? Can this be done through the activities and movement required during a game? I think so, if you have the right parties in the conversation developing those options.

Using music to bring kids into the classroom and adding aerobics, dance, sports . . . it doesn't matter how they move, they just need to move. If we offer options that have them move in ways they enjoy, they will want to do it often. We will incorporate movement breaks into every 90 minutes of schooltime.

My personal example of the impact of making movement part of a game came last year when our health insurance company offered an Apple Watch to members 50 and older. The insured could keep the watch at a discounted rate in exchange for a commitment to burn at least 300 calories per day. Miss that 300-calorie goal, and we would pay a higher price that month for the watch. I found myself feverishly exercising at the end of the day in order to meet that goal, if I had forgotten to wear the watch all day.

The point here is that when there is an incentive, even when the engaged don't remember what the reward or repercussions entail, there is motivation. I cannot remember anything about the cost I would pay if I missed the calorie goal, but I did remember the 300 calories. The goal of the health insurance company was to keep their members healthy by keeping them moving. And 300 calories a day isn't much, but it represents significant movement for a demographic that spends a lot of the day sitting at a desk.

Most of the research on brain health and nutrition deals with the predicted deficit when a child is malnourished or deprived of nutrients during those important developmental years. If that research were to be turned upside down and viewed from a Maslow perspective, we might conclude that in providing for nutrient needs and training good sleep habits, you could nurture strong-minded, well-considered individuals.

Could we nurture a generation ready to use science to evaluate their health? Could we nurture empathy and encourage a generation of young people who have an appreciation for facts and a respect for others' opinions about health science? If we can, perhaps we can begin to move the culture in the direction of fact-based conversations.

I'd like to suggest a good read that sums up a good deal of the research on this subject: *Brain Rules* by John Medina.[5] This book conveys the results of multiple research papers in a well-written narrative accessible to everyone. Medina presents a way of thinking about brain development that could positively influence curriculum development. We will get back to *Brain Rules* later in the book.

TURNING NUTRITION AND EXERCISE INTO A GAME

Is it possible to positively impact nutrition and exercise routines through games? I think so. Is the learning less impressive if the student gained the knowledge in a game? I think not. If kids learn math to be able to play or create a video game, is that less impressive than learning math for the sake of learning

continued

---

5   John Medina, "Brain Rules," Brain Rules.net, accessed December 19, 2021, https://brainrules.net/brain-rules/.

math? If our ultimate goal is to inspire a love of learning (and I believe it is), we would be wise to pay attention to what students want to be doing on a daily basis and then to create a curriculum from there.

Students need motivation, and it is our job as the adults in the room to help them find their interests so that motivation is a natural reaction. Some of the games will involve aerobic movement; some will require a basic understanding of nutrition and sleep. We owe it to our children to make sure they establish lifelong healthy habits with regard to nutrition and sleep. How we accomplish that should be based on what works, not on what we have always done.

My son, who is now an adult, heard me tell him to stop playing video games and get to his homework more times than I want to admit. I believe students' level of engagement would increase substantially if the experience of education were closer to the students' interests.

A decade or so ago there was a game that hit the market called Dance Dance Revolution. Surprisingly, kids lost weight while playing it because they were so engrossed in the game. A young, fit, 16-year-old was a regular guest on the morning-show circuit because she lost 90 pounds as a result of the game. This laser-focused, high-engagement game is exactly how we should be designing educational games.

BUSINESS SKILLS AND ENTREPRENEURSHIP

Schools should give kids who are interested a chance to run a business and gain a firsthand economic understanding of commerce. Students would engage, through various levels of sophistication, in their versions of the lemonade stand. I use that as an example because it is relatable and without controversy. Most of us have attempted a lemonade stand at some point. The difference here is that the student would be planning, budgeting, taking care of prep work, and actually taking the product to market—setting up that lemonade stand or storefront or offering whatever their invention is to the market. And imagine if all the hard and soft skills needed to be successful in this business (and in life) were being taught through video games. Why not?

And what if students invented products and had the opportunity to register a patent? What if they were helped to set up their own enterprise and manage funds, materials, or intellectual property? What if we helped kids understand all this while they were still in school?

Very young children could be setting up their version of an actual lemonade stand for their family or their classmates. As the student's interests develop, so could the complexity of the venture they are creating. In the most engaged students we might see patents and/or business licenses become part of the curriculum. Other students might try something

continued

that doesn't work—so no huge investment lost to gain wisdom—and develop the grit that comes from experiencing those setbacks.

Planning for a career the way it was done in the 1950s is no longer an option. If we help children understand the transactional nature of adult life while they are still in school—with supervision and support—it could help them prepare for a career in any field. I propose that it could offer a healthy perspective of the multiple priorities competing for your time and resources as an adult. I'm convinced that the majority of this can be done in a gamified curriculum. Kids are already learning these skills when they are gathering resources in their favorite game. A video game can nurture the skills needed for any entrepreneurial venture. We aren't being asked to invent something from scratch. We need to take the successful items in video games that students are already excited about and add content that drives interest in the area educators need covered.

STUDENTS AS PRODUCTIVE
MEMBERS OF SOCIETY

COVID-19 has taught us plenty: High on the list is the fact that we need to prepare for the unexpected. The majority of children in elementary school today—the kids who are living through this pandemic—will work at jobs that don't yet exist. There is a significant debate in the education community about what percentage that will be, but there is no question, the number will be significant. We need this next generation to prepare for a world of change. We need them to be problem solvers and entrepreneurs to take on the challenges and opportunities facing their generation.

We will need government support to make this happen. Not just the Department of Education. We need tax benefits offered to the game-design community if they add standards-aligned educational elements to their most popular games. We also need to compensate educators for building out the content needed in games that address curriculum. There could be financial rewards down the road for the companies, but at the moment there is little incentive for them to take time away from more profitable fantasy game play to address educational elements. However, we don't have time to wait for long-term profits to get this effort underway. The pandemic has cost students hundreds of hours and days of instruction. In order to make up for that loss, we need programs that hook the students' interest and slip the educational content into the system seamlessly.

This is an appealing area for research. Can children learn relevant skills for evaluating information and understand systems used in the adult experience of industry while still enjoying and celebrating childhood, or is it prohibitive to a healthy and happy childhood?

This is not a completely unique idea. The Junior Achievement program and others have been doing this in the after-school space for generations. The question Nolan asks is why should these essential learning opportunities be relegated to after school when they offer such rich opportunities to engage students in acquiring key skills and learnings that will have value in every area of their lives?

In an ideal school setting, this would be a significant portion of the school curriculum. The question this forces us to ask is what do we see as the purpose of education?

TRIAL AND ERROR AT EACH STAGE

Nolan's position is that school is best when it is designed to prepare the child for the realities of their life as an adult. This carries sway in part because of the eight-person research group known as the Bushnell kids. All are adults now, and they are engaged, curious, and active individuals. The question that remains unanswered but worthy of consideration and research is: can we prepare the child for adult life while making room for them to still enjoy the important elements of childhood?

In the current system of educating, we fill the students with facts and figures, hoping they recall the answer for a test. What Nolan is proposing is trial and error at every stage. The ability to conduct real-time and longitudinal studies in this environment offers multiple opportunities. And it will offer the data needed to make broad changes in education.

There is value in helping students understand that each failure or setback informs a future success. Few children in school today would say they see failure as helpful. Yet there is great benefit in allowing children to make mistakes and learn from them. If a student is interested in commerce and has an idea for a start-up, the school infrastructure could be the safest space to try out their ideas. The need to research, write a compelling description of the idea and ensuing project, design a business plan with budgets, and build a prototype or artistic representation of the idea hits on multiple disciplines.

Tough lessons might be easier to digest when there are coaches and teachers there to help evaluate and explore the learning in the experience. The student's writing skills, their critical thinking and problem-solving skills, and their ability to research will all be put to the test and will improve as a result of the effort. The student will have explored through research what is currently available about their idea. Ultimately, we want the student to celebrate each experience as a success or a setback and acknowledge the value in the setbacks that led them to where they are.

My oldest son, Brent, sold chocolate bars for his school and tickets to school events, and he sold them to gain points toward the prizes he could win if he was top seller. Brent often refers to those experiences as informative in his current role in designing, planning, and opening the Two Bit Circus Micro Amusement Park in the Arts District of Los Angeles. He credits those early years of setting goals and working hard to meet them with the grit and determination he has needed to get through tough times. I don't think he sees any of this experience as detrimental to his ability to enjoy his childhood.

TEACH CREATIVE PROBLEM-SOLVING SKILLS

We need to encourage teachers and school districts to adapt from lecture-style teaching to learning by doing. What child would choose a day of sitting still and taking notes over the

continued

option of working in a makerspace? Would students choose to make something or reverse-engineer a motor or an appliance over sitting and listening to someone describe the activity while they take notes? So many standard lessons can be taught by engaging students in an activity or game. My parenting was all done around projects. My kids knew they could get me involved and I them, through presenting a challenge or a project. I didn't buy them the latest anything to work with; I gave them access to tools and materials.

What Nolan is suggesting is high on every teacher's list of goals with his or her students. The challenge is finding a way to make it meaningful to a room full of students with different interests, talents, and ideas who are all starting at different levels of skill. It is essential that we begin to address this early in their education, but this has not proven to be simple.

In the debate about what percentage of elementary students will be working at jobs that don't yet exist, there is no argument about the reality, only the percentage. Robots will do the follow-the-directions jobs of the future. What we need are creative and critical thinkers and problem solvers to lead the charge facing the issues of their day. You don't want 20th-century game plans for 21st-century issues. We can safely assume that the majority of the current elementary students will need to be prepared for realities that are yet to be experienced along with the obvious issues we are leaving for them to face concerning the environment.

So much of what we do in our culture is done because "it is the way we have always done it." Yet we are facing a future with environmental challenges, health concerns, and food insecurity and nutritional deficiencies. Many of these problems will require righting systems and rethinking the way we have always done it. To accomplish that, we need problem solvers, and problem-solving starts with creative thinking.

Sylvia Libow Martinez and Gary Stager, PhD, in *Invent to Learn*,[6] offer a rallying cry for this pedagogy. Children learn while doing (you name the task), provided they are interested in the task. What the interest or the task involves isn't as important as the fact that they are engaged. Our job is to discover what the child is interested in, and once we know that, we have the potential to keep them engaged in exploration of that interest and more.

We can buy kids expensive robotics kits, but I recommend we don't. With an expensive kit, the student learns to make a robot by following the instructions. That may be fun for the time of the build, but it doesn't inspire critical thinking or problem-solving the way a noninstructed exploration or build would. The designer took that informative struggle out of the experience by sharing the instructions with the student in the form of step-by-step directions.

In our work with children, our approach is to give kids random materials that can be reused, like cardboard, plastic widgets of all shapes and colors, wood, fabric, overstock or industrial mistakes, you name it. (If there was an error in a container factory process, and a lid doesn't fit its container, that's the kind of thing that can be found in our warehouse.) We include an Arduino-inspired board when that is needed and appropriate to the student's skill set.[7] With this, the student can program, maybe add some old motors . . . and design and create a robot. This requires problem-solving, which helps hone those critical-thinking

---

6   "About the Book," Invent to Learn.com, accessed December 19, 2021, https://inventtolearn.com/about-the-book/.

7   Arduino is an open-source electronics platform based on easy-to-use hardware and software. Arduino boards are able to read inputs—light on a sensor, a finger on a button, or a Twitter message—and turn it into an output —activating a motor, turning on an LED, publishing something online. (Source: "What is Arduino?" Arduino, accessed July 7, 2022, https://www.arduino.cc/en/Guide/Introduction).

and creative skills. It requires making an adjustment each time an idea doesn't work. These are the skills and experiences that will serve students in any career or life challenge for the balance of their life.

EXAMPLES OF SUCCESS

As evidence of the effectiveness of this approach, I submit the team that inspired the 2015 film called *Spare Parts*. This group of undocumented high school students with no experience in robotics took an $800 investment they acquired by dismantling a used car for its parts—selling some of the parts and using others in their creation—and went up against the well-funded winners from the previous year, which included teams from MIT, Stanford, Cornell, and other top universities that were also a part of the competition.

These four high school students created an underwater robot for the competition, though they had never seen the ocean. And they were the first high school students to enter the college category. It didn't stop there; to everyone's shock, they won the competition. What happened as a result of that win was clear in the impact it had on other students in the community. The school continued to enter the competition yearly and won the next two consecutive years. At ExoDexa we often repeat, "If you can see it, you can be it." These four students made it clear that effort and dedication can beat out a thick wallet. In fact, as mentioned earlier, it might be an advantage not to have the money to fix every problem as it arises.

Here's another example: Kelvin Doe, a young man from Sierra Leone, wanted to create a radio station. But his village often had power outages and could only count on electricity for a few hours a week. Without power he couldn't run the station, and no one could hear him, either. So he created batteries out of material he recovered from the landfill near where he lives. His creation, and his radio persona, DJ Focus, garnered him enough attention that an MIT student arranged to bring Kelvin to Boston to spend a summer at MIT. After that summer of learning and experimenting with new tools and materials, he was eager to return to his community and share everything he had learned. He was able to show those back home a pathway to invention.

Easy access to money often doesn't create space for creativity, and it certainly doesn't inspire creative problem-solving. If you have the money, you solve the problem by purchasing what you need. If you don't have the money, you consider all the possibilities, you problem solve, and you create.

Some students are motivated on their own, and others rely on the educator's creativity to help them find their interest. Once the interest is discovered, it is our role as educators to help them remain curious. The student can build the resilience that will be required for any venture or career if the right habits are established early. This is one of the jobs we as educators take seriously.

HAVE A SCHOOL DAY FREE FROM BOREDOM

There is plenty of research that tells us kids learn best when they are fully engaged. And, again, the secret to full engagement lies in understanding the child's interest. Keeping them engaged requires that we keep the child's curiosity levels high. Achieving this also requires that we leave room for exploration of their interests and add new interests based on what is discovered in the process. Also, the flow of work needs to be in line with both the child's and the educators' expectations.

Until recently, that was a difficult—some would say impossible—task. Much of the burden fell on the teacher, and as we've noted, when you have 25–35 students in the room it is hard to be aware of what ignites each child. Now with online options and hidden testing capabilities, we can determine pretty quickly what the student is interested in and offer them more opportunities to dig deeply into that. We can also expand their knowledge base within that interest while trying to expose them to broader ideas and concepts.

How different would the experience of school be if kids had a say in how their day is set up? Of course kids would spend most of the day on games, so why not make sure those games are loaded with hidden education, games that require students to engage in research to answer questions that will get them to the next level or allow them to purchase equipment needed for the next level.

Recently, our board president, Malik Ducard, who was a senior executive at YouTube for a decade and is now at Pinterest, told me that he made the internet log-ins for his sons' favorite platforms all different math equations. He told his sons that they had to solve the equation if they wanted access to Netflix or any of their other favorite accounts. What a great way to make math meaningful! The boys had to focus on a problem and work out the answer—sometimes together, sometimes in competition—but the bottom line is they were practicing problem-solving.

If we could make sure the students are playing games that drive interest and build a knowledge base in history, math, music, and literature, all without feeling like they are being educated, we might stand a chance at engaging them, even with their common distractions. We could have systems that can address what Nolan is calling for with a school free of boredom.

There is an opportunity to involve older children in developing learning games for younger students. To truly learn something, one should teach it to someone else. A 15-year-old will relate more closely to the desires and interests of a 7-year-old than a 30-year-old will. What if 15-year-olds were designing games for 7-year-olds? Not only would that anchor the learning for the 15-year-old, the process could become a source of income. Some of these games could become the base for that 15-year-old's business. If the game were to prove useful beyond of the original need, there is a further market in other schools, districts, and informal education outlets. Khan Academy started as a mentoring project that the young professional Sal Khan was conducting to help his younger cousins with math struggles.

We could also build movement into the games, so that even when the child doesn't take an official break every 60–90 minutes, they are still moving to accomplish a goal in the game.

Game designers have managed to captivate children with the help of psychologists. We need to adapt those designs to help kids engage and take ownership of their learning. The idea of having a school day free of boredom would be a welcome reality for teachers as well as students.

CHAPTER 4

Instill Optimism and Enthusiasm

Educators see that we have a generation of students who seem frightened to try anything new. These students are fearful of failure and unlikely to embrace projects and topics that are not at least somewhat familiar. This is not true of kindergartners. Sir Ken Robinson spoke of a longitudinal research project done in Britain starting with kindergartners; 98 percent of the 1,500 children in the study tested at the genius level for creativity at age five. They were then tested every few years until they were in their late teens, and every set of tests showed a diminished ability to think creatively. Sir Ken made the point that we are literally educating the creativity out of children.

If we find a child's interest and help them explore it, we will have created an environment that can usher in a lifetime of creativity and curiosity and is indeed necessary to inspire research.

Optimism and enthusiasm are informed by creativity. We think creatively when we believe an idea is achievable. We become enthusiastic about things we are passionate about, and we become more creative as we barrel ahead, working on issues that are relevant to our interests and interesting for us to work on. If a child is optimistic, they see a mistake or failure as a minor setback. If the child lacks optimism, a setback can become the end of the line on a project that really just needed a few adjustments and a little more time.

Life is a series of challenges with plateaus, peaks, and valleys between those challenges. Helping students develop an optimistic view of themselves, their education, and their ability to excel in difficult situations will serve them well as students and beyond.

We work in hundreds of local schools and with educators around the world. We see concern about an issue that is being debated in academic circles everywhere: How do we instill a can-do attitude in students? How do we help the child understand that "can do" often means that you can do it with a lot of practice, experimentation, and minor or major setbacks and failures along the way. Some progressive educators have begun to celebrate failures in class and use those to explore the lessons learned from the failure in a way that honors the child who took the risk and tried something new.

According to Henry Ford, "The only real failure is the one you fail to learn from." We wholeheartedly agree.

Every effective researcher knows that they will fail far more often than they succeed, but that each failure informs a future success. If our medical community were stopped by their failures, we would never have had effective vaccines or treatments for disease. To fail means you are trying new things, moving outside of your comfort zone, and that is where we find some of our best failures and some of the finest successes.

> Our students will be encouraged to fail and to share the stories of the failure with each other in an effort to spread knowledge and help others feel safe exploring when the outcome is uncertain. Students will be rewarded for writing up their failure and documenting their learning so that it is instilled in them and available as a resource for other students. The idea is to make it easy for students to try and fail and try again with new information.

The move toward learning by doing requires training for educators and also requires resources. Kids need material to build with and to experiment with, and educators need training on how to guide this process without directing it. For Two Bit Circus Foundation, this means using upcycled material (in other words, material that would be in a landfill if we weren't rescuing it) and putting it into the hands of students for their prototypes. Because of the nature of our materials, it's okay to start over, reusing what you can and finding replacement parts for what you can't reuse. We aren't working with expensive kits and materials that make it prohibitive for students to simply start over if something doesn't work the way they had planned.

With individualized education a possibility, engaging each student in studies they are interested in becomes a reasonable expectation of the education system. That is half the battle. If you have the student's interest, you can help them educate themselves by following their interest down the rabbit hole. Optimism and enthusiasm are natural offshoots of personal discoveries and achievements.

IF ONE'S TALENT ISN'T
OBVIOUS, KEEP LOOKING

One of my sons was often bored in the classroom. He had the top marks in most classes but found no joy in the educational process. In one class in particular, biology, he was consistently the top-scoring student on quizzes except for one time when he was second. At the end of the semester, however, he received a D for the class. He was understandably frustrated and wanted an explanation. The teacher acknowledged that my son had a firm grasp on the content but noted that he had not handed in the mandatory homework. My son thought of the homework as busywork and not worthy of his time, since he knew the material well enough to ace the tests. The teacher was firm on her requirement for the homework to be handed in and on time. This was the end of my son's interest in high school. Was it on him or on the system to adjust?

In our school, students will be required to gain understanding. How they gain it and demonstrate it will be up to the student and their mentors, but rigid rules that alienate the learner will not be part of the system.

The problem that Nolan describes for his son is not unusual. School has been established around rigid rules that require all students to follow the instructions and rules without consideration for level of understanding or obvious accomplishment of the end goal by a different route. We change the way students see themselves by forcing round pegs into square holes. Not every child has a Bushnell parent to help navigate the system. As a result, students often blame themselves for what isn't working.

So many students by middle school don't see themselves as having any particular talent. If you were to ask a group in kindergarten what they think are their best talents, they would list them with enthusiasm. This is part of the reason that Sir Ken Robinson can tell us that 90-plus percent of kindergarteners tested as genius on the creativity tests. Along with damaging their sense of themselves as creative through standard education, it seems we are also removing confidence about their particular talents.

Many adults are left with the same diminished self-image. For educators, the most important part of the job is to find the hidden talents and encourage the student to follow the information about their talent and interests through time zones, eras, geography, and political movements. We can help the child discover their talent through the study of their interest and the exploration of human needs. This fits my personal philosophy as an educator, but it isn't original to me. Programs founded by Waldorf (1919) and Emilia Reggio (1945) have used this approach in formal and informal education with considerable success for decades. In the case of Waldorf, it's been more than a century of success.

Often when a child is naturally good at something, or something comes to them quickly, they don't think of that as talent. They consider it easy and therefore somehow less valuable. It is in everyone's best interest to help the child recognize their talent regardless of the difficulty or ease with which they engage in it. When they begin to see something particular to them as a talent, they may be more interested in exploring who else has this talent, where it is applied by others, and what kind of careers are possible with it. And once you have them asking those questions, you can introduce them to the history of the people or discoveries relevant to their talent. The talent is a pathway for the child to take control of their studies, and it is up to us to honor their interest by asking questions that send them on their path of discovery.

KEEP OPEN TO EXPLORATION

How do we marry this search for talent to our previous interest in avoiding boredom? The best way to ensure that students are not bored is to offer them the opportunity to explore areas in which they already have demonstrated interest. History can be taught to a student through whatever their interests entail. A student keen on music can learn about the political system that assisted or hindered the careers of their musical role model or person of interest. It is our job to ask questions that will have students wanting to research issues around their interests. The burden is then on the person who will gain the most from the research—the student—to explore those interests. There is no need for the educator to know all of the information on the topic in advance. In our current system, the teacher knows the subject and teaches it to the student. That is passive, ineffective, and doesn't nurture the student's curiosity.

Through questioning we can easily find a way to interweave the interests of the student with the standards we as educators need to cover. Beyond this, our system will assure the student is prepared for higher education and/or career opportunities. Each child has talents; it is our responsibility to help them discover, appreciate, and grow with those talents.

INTRODUCING THE NINE KEY
PRINCIPLES OF THE EXODEXA MODEL

STRATEGIES AND TACTICS

In order to instill optimism and enthusiasm and prepare students for higher education and career choices, changes are needed. This is where the new strategies and tactics become essential.

New tactics added to an old system won't work, however. Disruptive change is what is needed in education. This kind of change usually requires a complete redesign of the workday and workflow. Our strategies will include just that: a redesign of the building and the class schedule. Sitting kids in rows or at tables based on their age is an archaic system. If we are to batch kids for study, let's batch them by interest rather than age. A seven-year-old interested in aerospace should be the junior member of the team looking at aerospace. But perhaps batching kids isn't the best system for learning anyway. We only batch kids when they decide to work together on a project.

What follows is the first of nine principles—strategies and tactics—that we believe will get us to a place where kids are making choices about their education, from how it is delivered to who delivers it to each student. The rest of the key strategies and tactics will be interspersed throughout the remaining chapters.

PRINCIPLE #1.
TEACH THROUGH GAMIFIED
LEARNING MODULES

We start with modules and games that can be customized to the student and delivered online. These are recursive, provide a schema, and track progress, creating a mind map for the student that is refreshed at intervals in order to convert short-term memory into long-term understanding.

Kids simply do not write enough, but it is understood that

continued

today's English teachers are reluctant to assign essays since 35 students in each of five or six classes create lost weekends of correcting papers.

By moving a lot of learning into software, we can free up time for teachers to focus on a few students and give deep, meaningful feedback to their writing.

If we can solve the issue of time by outsourcing both learning and correction to software and, in doing so, free up the teacher to give learners creative and instant feedback, we are again making significant progress. A software program also removes the teacher bias that can happen when a teacher's expectations affect their grading.

Teaching through gamified learning modules could be an effective way of collecting data. It can also offer coaches, mentors, and educators the ability to adjust in real time, based on the student's engagement and areas of interest. For the last couple of decades, people have been working toward the development of digital resources and expanding their ability to offer measurement tools for digital curriculum with varying degrees of success. Nolan's interest in using his programs as a research laboratory will offer a meaningful way to conduct longitudinal research to test the theory. It also offers a school the ability to adjust quickly if something isn't effective.

The enemy of the gamified approach to education is the classroom as it currently exists. We know a great deal about what isn't working: Not all children are effective at note taking and memorizing facts, but they can create, invent, and problem solve all day. Our current system is leaving a great many students without an effective education by ignoring these facts. And we have not made significant enough change to deal with that problem.

The one-to-many delivery system of information, imparted at a single speed to a passive group of students is not only old fashioned, it's also not effective. It has the further disadvantage of being boring to some and baffling to others. Both groups become disengaged, often becoming disruptive and creating additional problems for the class. On a computer, students can be engaged in a lesson that is tailored to his or her interests and delivered at their ideal speed. There's no time to be bored and no shame no matter how long it takes to complete a module. That's between the student and their computer.

Prepandemic education in the classroom belongs in the history books. And now, as a result of the pandemic, we can address the need for change, using what we know works and losing what we know does not work. In a digital-curriculum world we can address the need for change in the moment, as we become aware of the needs of each child as an individual rather than as part of a batch.

Students sitting and taking notes from a lecturing teacher has never been the best way to inspire kids. Brain science tells us that we learn best when we are active. But active does not simply mean moving; it means doing, making decisions, and experimenting, followed by evaluation, testing, and starting again. A digital curriculum can supply this environment on an individual basis in a way that the classroom alone has not.

A computer can also offer many strategies not available to the traditional classroom. The computer will provide a schema that has been proven in video games and other research to enhance engagement and memory. The software can also track the student's knowledge. It can create a complete inventory of what a student knows and a probable decay profile alerting us to what information they are not able to maintain over time. It can then, based on the student's experience, time the reviews properly to ensure retention.

Research has shown that turning short-term memory into long-term knowledge requires repetition, and the timing of the repetition is key to locking in memory. Review is most effective if spaced over time, with the first review coming about two hours after the first introduction. A second review after a good night's sleep has also shown effectiveness.

Many students will continue with modules beyond the required learning, becoming more and more advanced. High school students may take college-level subjects as a result of the continued time spent on their interests and modules. This will start to blur the line as to what constitutes high school and what is college. It also sets up a habit of learning in chunks that can be repeated at any age, intergenerationally, with any interest.

A proper school system should inspire learning "K through gray," that is, throughout one's life. What a different world we would have if everyone were engaged in lifelong learning. These modules, with essential teaching assistance, could indicate a student's learning accomplishments as they grow older.

Beyond high school, module reports will indicate a potential employee's strengths and interests to an employer. Since the modules are self-testing and remedial to previous modules, the more recent the module in a subject indicates that the student has mastered the material and is also familiar with what has come before. Most employers lean toward hiring a curious individual and regular module user over someone who has not felt it important to upgrade skills since formal school ended.

After completion of a module, the student can walk around or shift activity. Difficult subjects can be interspersed with easier or less taxing subjects.

In our system we never present any information or a process for which the student lacks preparation. The review system keeps information in one's memory and also ensures that no subject is taught without the prerequisite knowledge. It does this without embarrassment or ridicule in front of classmates. This bite-size learning with all the foundational work available allows the student to see each leap of understanding as natural and easy. What is basically a brain inventory database for each student will guide them and constantly challenge and refresh their accumulated learning.

This system has multiple advantages for the student as well as for the institution to monitor the success and long-term impact of the learning modules. It also prevents anyone from moving on to new data before the earlier data is fully understood, a situation that currently causes frustration and can lead to a larger problem later, when the student fails to understand crucial foundational material. This is particularly true in subjects that require sound bases, such as engineering and mathematics, among others.

The ability to track the progress of the student and gauge their level of interest and commitment in real time offers rich research opportunities.

In most cases the modules should take about 15 minutes to complete. Research shows that students seldom can stay fully engaged in a subject for longer than that, so our approach is to take the student as far as they can move on a subject in 15-minute intervals. Student engagement is a powerful precursor to learning and remembering. In test after test, most students are disengaged with a lecture after 15 minutes, and that is often when the discipline problems become more of an issue.

The more of our senses that can be engaged, the better we remember. The modules rely heavily on visuals and animation. The brain loves visuals with motion and meaning. That is just how the brain works.

Keeping the modules to 15 minutes will also offer students the ability to jump into subjects while they are interested and engaged. That way they can continue with that subject and satisfy their curiosity as well as the requirements.

Certainly Nolan's point about engaging multiple senses is backed up by research. The more senses, and the more firing neurons, the better the ability to recall the experience and the information present. Adding taste and smell can significantly impact recall. Text-only lessons are the easiest to forget and require much more review.

The data gained through this exploration will inform us about each student's interests. The curriculum can then be placed within a framework relevant to those. With this data we can create a schema that meets each student within their range of interests. Once a student is studying within that range, it becomes easier for them to process information and then to understand and remember the information and the experience. We can, during these dives into interest, offer windows into other relevant fields of study.

SMELL-A-VISION MODULES

There was a computer peripheral several years ago that was linked to some video games. It was a little box that connected to a USB port that would emit one of eight smells under program control. The device could emit rose, pine, coffee, baking bread, and several other aromas. If a student learns something with an accompanying smell, that student can recall the lesson with amazingly higher accuracy if the same smell is present. The same thing happens if the student is walking when learning a lesson; recall is better with the movement. Also, if there is a problem with recall, you can repeat the behavior. In other words, if the student is walking later, that movement can trigger the recall.

continued

The diversity of software lessons allows a student to browse many subjects on a cursory level to create curiosity. It can also lead the student into deeper and more difficult or nuanced levels. Imagine a student being able to plunge into advanced placement (AP), college, or even PhD levels of difficulty seamlessly. If the child shows aptitude and interest, we should offer that avenue. On the other end of the scale, subjects that are difficult for some can be made more remedial so that each subject becomes attainable at some level.

Engaging, and at times, protecting the senses could be especially helpful for students who tend to be fidgety. In a classroom of 30–35 students, it isn't possible to be as flexible as one can be if the students are in self-guided study. Nolan has the students wearing noise-canceling headsets, which offer some autonomy to the student focused on their studies as well as independence to the student who needs to get up and move often.

As with growth spurts, some students may have periods of intense focus during which they may drill down on an area of interest and accomplish work that is beyond their age-related grade level. If they have the prerequisite knowledge, there is no reason to slow them down. This is also an area that could excite educational-research professionals.

As learning by doing or making has become key to student engagement, working in a STEAM Lab Makerspace (SLM) can be a reward for effort in required modules. As previously mentioned, state requirements will need to be addressed in this system; they just don't need to be addressed in lecture style. Completing a learning module on tool safety and makerspace cooperative work culture will be required to allow access to the SLM equipment. No one will be able to use the laser cutter or other tools in the SLM without finishing the module that considers safety issues and describes its operation. Our mission is to make learning engaging so the student works far beyond what they had intended or expected.

It is challenging to try to address 30–35 students at a time. What works for one student is a nightmare for another. If a teacher is frustrated with the pace of the class because some students can't keep up, that can paralyze the slower students and slow down the students who are absorbing the material more quickly. Communicating without anger or ambiguity offers the information in a manner that the student can hear and fit into their worldview.

We know that teaching and learning require effective communication, but to accomplish that, we need to know the student. The more effectively we can communicate to a student within their interests, the better the chance our message will land on fertile soil.

Step-by-step we build understanding and give teachers the room to know the students. Once there is a bond, it is easier to encourage a student when needed and give space to another when that is required.

Particular attention will be paid in the software to ensure that the student does not leap over lessons not previously learned.

continued

A new level will open up to the student only as they complete (with accuracy) each prerequisite module. And this will be done with acknowledgment only by the involved student and not with the judgment of other students or teaching staff.

REDUCING BIAS IN THE CLASSROOM

There is a great deal of public discourse about institutional bias regarding race. The ExoDexa style of teaching has potential to mitigate this issue. It could also have an impact on implicit bias, since, as Nolan points out, the system adapts according to individual needs, not generalized assumptions about how the student should learn.

Gamified learning modules, as Nolan describes them, are flexible and can be modified for students regardless of their learning preference. They offer much-needed insight and understanding to teachers, parents, and anyone interested in progressive education. All the modules would be constantly tested for efficacy, with an initial quality-assurance period that can be addressed in the first schools offered licenses in the research pods. Nolan is offering the software and learning system to select schools as a starting point for the needed research.

A module that teaches faster and better with less teacher intervention would offer educators the time and space to focus on the development of a young learner, rather than delivering information in a uniform way to a batch of students put together because of their birth dates rather than their interests.

In a school based on gamified learning modules delivered through software, the teachers would be freed up to work as coaches and mentors to students. I enjoyed the relationships I was able to build with some students and faculty while I was a university professor. The challenge was the lack of time to truly connect with my students. I do know that everyone I spoke with could point to an educator or after-school mentor who positively influenced their self-image or their interest in their studies or a career. Sometimes it was someone who influenced each of those areas.

Everyone I've met who is successful had someone in that role in their life. Having a system that honors this reality would benefit the students. Having teachers who are less overwhelmed with teaching the curriculum and more engaged in supporting a student's exploration and documentation of how the curriculum intersects, or doesn't, with their lived experiences would greatly enhance the student's experience.

TRACKING PROGRESS

Everyone likes to know where they are as they progress toward a goal. In the video game world this is especially true. Leveling up, histograms, completing a field, and breaking all the bricks are all about completing a level or task. Completion is satisfying, and tracking progress toward completion is further satisfying. Associated with each module is a series of indicators that track progress through the subject.

Sometimes it is fun to complete a task that is almost done. At other times we may prefer to add options of things to work on at any given time. Some students like tasks one at a time; others want to move back and forth from one task to another.

continued

Feeling the freedom to dive deep into a subject on a whim can be rewarding. This can often lead to a cleanup mode, where getting tasks off your plate becomes important. Several puzzle games use this metric to keep people engaged with great success: Work on something for a while, get stuck, work on something else. Often the brain continues processing in the background, and upon return the problem vanishes. Histograms—progress bars—are a great indicator of progress. Color coding further enhances the experience.

The late Tony Buzan made a career out of helping people hold things in their memory longer by enlisting the help of colors. His mind mapping was developed as an effective tool for note taking, but the research on his process offers insight into the effectiveness of color added to studies in general.

Salting the mine—adding extra value in the early stages of a process—is an old trick used in many marketing plans, amusement parks, Las Vegas, and video games. It works like this: The most difficult task psychologically is starting a project that will take a long time to complete. Often people are overwhelmed by the perceived enormousness of the job before them. Modules are a way of breaking that daunting school year into bite-size chunks, but there are also some other great tricks that have a substantial track record for success.

Most of us have has been given a punch card at a coffee house or dry cleaner. These typically have a bunch of numbers or symbols around the edge and promise the holder that upon completing a number of punches or stamps they will earn a free coffee or a free dry cleaning. Usually there are ten punch holes, and the barista or shop owner punches the first one and hands you the card. Merchants have learned, though, that if the card has 12 punch holes and is handed to the customer with the clerk's having punched out three holes, the number of cards redeemed more than doubles.

What is the difference? It is all in the perception of the customer. With three punches out, it seems you have made more progress toward a goal. In fact, both cards have nine punches left, but you feel closer to the end goal.

Keeping this punch-card theory in mind, our modules could start with a test of several questions, and the histogram at the bottom will begin to fill. This indicates that you have already made some progress. At this point the subject that has sparked your curiosity will spur you on the way. The fact that the histogram thermometer is now partially filled in is rewarding and builds enthusiasm, often when it is most needed. The speed of fill is also nonlinear. Early on, progress is inflated, so that when a module is 25 percent complete, the histogram will appear almost half filled. Progress slows as the module approaches completion or when the goal is in sight. At this point, little encouragement is needed. Slot machines have used this technique for years with extremely positive results.

continued

Educators rarely use Las Vegas as a North Star, but I can see effective motivation for a student in the way Nolan outlines the idea of salting the mine. It is true that many students of any age find the beginning of a project the most terrifying. Procrastination and avoidance are the preferred methods of many when it comes to writing a paper or starting a project. It's hard to admit this, but salting the mine may be an effective solution for this dilemma in student work. I'm in favor of anything that gives the student a feeling of accomplishment early in an endeavor.

This also eliminates the comparative approach to school grading. When a student needs a push, the system can address that need without embarrassment. The ability to push through or take a break is there for each student.

In this modular approach to education, we can keep educators as engaged as students. We can reach out to the best teachers in each subject and bring them to tens of thousands of students, something that in-person instruction doesn't allow. One of the benefits that this educational approach has for teachers is the automation of the tedious work that is an important part of education but not of teaching. We will focus more on this later, but taking attendance, marking papers, and compiling progress reports on academics will all be automated.

The teacher will have time to comment on development, interests, talents, and social structures that the student is engaged in or struggling with. Teachers want to teach. We think the system needs to honor that and make room for it without clouding the day with administrative tasks easily done by software.

CHAPTER 5

The Roles of Staff, Mentors, and the Student's Home

PRINCIPLE #2.
HAVE INSTANT ACCESS TO TEACHERS, COACHES, AND MENTORS

The need for engaging with a student on any particular subject happens only when the module fails to grant understanding. Mentors and educators will be notified when a student is struggling with the same issues over and over. If this happens in their writing, personal intervention can be offered before frustration takes over.

In the instance of a student's being totally stumped, the software alerts a mentor to launch a video chat with the student. This instant intervention helps make sure that the student never feels overwhelmed for long.

continued

The curriculum is flexible and rigorous. In this system, grade levels become a meaningless distinction for the student, but they can be easily determined when needed for academic advancement to higher education. The school must fulfill the needs of standardized tests, which direct a minimum quantity of modules in targeted STEAM subjects, but if the system is as efficient as expected, students will have large blocks of time for exploratory learning and pursuit of their interests.

The modules for SAT preparation and AP modules for the college bound will be available, as will other, more vocational modules. Computer programming, mechanics, cooking—both for fun and commercially—are just a few of the richer options that will be available.

As an aside, if a student is not happy with a grade on a paper, they can request a second opinion.

Most teachers are teaching because of the possible impact on their students. They want an environment in which they can teach without the burden of correcting excessive amounts of papers, assigning grades, keeping track of who is handing in what, and filling out paperwork such as attendance logs and all the reports required by law. In the effective schools of the future, most of this drudgery will be removed from the teachers' responsibilities so teachers can teach. The system leaves them free to move among the students either virtually by way of the video link or physically.

The only need for in-person work will happen in the STEAM Lab Makerspace when that becomes possible. One-on-one is the best way to teach, and research bears this out.

We will recruit some of the best mathematicians, biologists, physicists, and specialists in as many fields as the students need. With an online service, the ability to aggregate the students who desire this level of coaching makes that possible. This contact with capable people can often be more important than the actual subject mentoring.

Kids who are slow to learn can benefit the most from this system. As we noted in Chapter 1, it is often difficult to find out exactly what the problem is with an individual student. Slow reading skills and social issues are just two possible explanations. Again, once we understand the student's issues, we can offer support and assignments that focus on their unique type of cognitive difficulty.

For students who require more contact than others, we can organize academic mentors, including active or retired teachers. That has proved to be effective with several of our young people.

Some might argue that the students who "waste a good deal of time before they actually get started on tackling the issues" may be working on the issues in a different way than we are used to witnessing and measuring. The child who appears to be wasting time may be doing mundane tasks with one part of the brain while they process and consider what they are up against in a paper or a task with a different part of the brain.

As evidence, I offer the earlier story from Sir Ken Robinson about Gillian Lynne, who needed to move to learn. I recently learned of a bird that flies across the ocean to migrate. They have nowhere to stop and rest, so they have trained their brain to sleep, one section at a time. With this adaptation, they can fly continuously until they reach the shore. We don't fully understand our brain's capacity, so it seems likely we have plenty to explore around motivation and conduct of students taking on a task.

KEEPING KIDS MOTIVATED

We are all capable of so much more. When the light of understanding dawns on a face, this is a hugely rewarding experience for an educator. When a student feels understood rather than chastised for behavior that doesn't fit the classroom expectations, they are validated rather than diminished. Teachers don't have time for this kind of classroom management in the average elementary, middle, or high school. Drudgery, which could be managed well by technology, rarely leaves the educator time on a daily basis to truly connect with the student. Seeing the possibility of change is what keeps me motivated.

What we are promoting is individualized learning that is not a burden to the teacher. This is revolutionary. We have the content, we know where to find the best history teacher in Europe, say, or the best science teacher in America or Canada. The goal is to turn the content into games and modules that will captivate the child and build the desire to advance to the next level, so that the child is driven by their own curiosity and interests.

As I've noted, our system provides a teacher instantly for one-on-one mentoring when a child is stuck or disengaged. The online system flags the problem and attaches the appropriate coach/teacher/mentor to the conversation with the student. This teacher arrives at exactly the point that help is needed. This timing is imperative since waiting breaks the focus on the problem. One-on-one attention help keeps the student engaged in the subject yet allows just the right amount of struggle to keep interest, spur curiosity, and build problem-solving muscles without frustrating the student so much that they leave the interest behind.

The link to the teacher is created instantly, either on demand from the student or when the system prompts it. The teacher is automatically selected because they are especially skilled in the subject that the student is pursuing, or the child may have identified the person as their preferred coach/mentor.

When students are learning in person, each of their cubicles should have a video camera and a boom microphone, and all students would wear over-the-ear noise-canceling headphones. In the virtual world the same setup is possible. The teacher has the same equipment. The teacher also has a series of monitors that have thumbnail images of what all of their students are engaged in. A teacher can observe what is going on with a student via a simple click.

The software sorts the students based on time since their last correct answer. This means that all the students shown along the top row are either struggling with a concept or are goofing off. The teacher can see the current screen and lesson the student is struggling with, as well as the question that was last missed.

continued

The teacher can choose to intervene, transfer images, or activate a virtual blackboard to assist the student. When a student needs a deeper understanding of a difficult problem, an instructor with that knowledge or skill set could be contacted by the system and matched with the student.

If a student wants help, the teacher is just a click away. If the teacher in the classroom is busy, the network searches for an available instructor. As any call center can show, with sufficient teachers wrangling a large number of students, the wait time for an available teacher can be structured to a few seconds. If a student has a particular favorite teacher, the student can request the teacher's next opening and move forward with a different learning module while they are waiting.

In any class there are students with wildly different learning styles, speeds, and aptitudes. Nolan's system allows specialists to be linked to particularly gifted students and also accommodates those with learning challenges. There are often kids in a school who understand mathematics or physics better than any of their teachers. The ability to provide experts for these students as well as specially trained teachers for those who are struggling would offer a dynamic change in education.

MENTORS WITH GAME

Some students resonate with younger teachers and others with older role models. Certain students learn better from a male, while others prefer females. There is some evidence from the video game world that some kids prefer a synthetic archetype, fully aware that the construct is illusory. When it comes to the mage in a medieval town—Superman, Batman, Yoda, among others—students may have such strong attachments to them that they suspend disbelief and choose one of these characters as a mentor for certain subjects.

Since the prime student-mentor contact is through the video link, a series of software tools allow a mentor to "put on a different face" and perhaps even adopt the lexicon and voice of the construct. This may sound strange and troubling to some, but in the world of the future we abandon preconceived notions of efficacy and seek what works the best. This is part of our "meet them where they are" philosophy. If learning from Batman makes education engaging for a student, let's put Batman in the classroom. For others it could be a respected sports hero. Who knows?

Allowing kids to have fun and changing their mentors when they see it as necessary may be an extra tool to encourage engagement. Children need a different voice at different stages and for different reasons. A child who has just experienced a family collapse through divorce will need a different mentor than the one who has qualified for the academic Olympics.

Many celebrities already support Boys and Girls Clubs, and other programs that help inner-city youth; they might be willing to lend their voice to a mentor avatar. And with the advent of holograms and augmented reality, we can bring past celebrities and inventors to life for a student. Wouldn't it be cool to learn screenwriting from Steven Spielberg, math from Albert Einstein, physics from Richard Feynman, economics from Milton Friedman, Civil War history from Abraham Lincoln, and about human rights issues from Martin Luther King Jr.?

That is becoming more feasible and could further motivate children to take agency over their education. I am not talking about showing a video of these people. Students could interact with a likeness of a figure that is actually being operated by a teacher; technology could mimic the speech patterns and syntax of the famous person. Software moves the lips of the construct in sync with the teacher, maintaining the illusion of reality. Even though all would know that the person behind the curtain is not the Wizard of Oz but someone more earthly, the effect could be interesting. Our hypothesis is that this would be more effective than traditional teaching methods at gaining the students' interest and positively impacting their retention of information.

An important aspect of our system is that students can shop for teachers. There is only a single reason to select one teacher over another: the ability to make information clear and understandable. The old categories of easy or hard teachers disappear. There is no place for a teacher who gives few good grades or assigns massive amounts of homework. In our system, grades and teachers are separated, so kids will stop looking for an easy teacher and instead gravitate toward the educator who can explain clearly and be of real help in areas where the student needs support. Learning the module is the objective; all the other factors have been removed. Over a few years the student may move from one mentor/teacher to another, depending on the student's needs during that stage of their education.

Teachers will have a built-in advantage over everyone else in module writing, since they will see which areas continue to be confusing to students. When they help a student over an obstacle, the teachers will quickly devise a modification that improves the module. Working teachers will become the best module writers, causing great leaps in the students' education. The teachers' finances will be positively impacted because they'll be writing modules. Systems that reward efficiency get more of it.

PRINCIPLE #3.
EMPHASIZE PROPER NUTRITION,
SLEEP, AND A LEARNING ATTITUDE

The body is a chemical engine that requires not only fuel but also the component parts to build brain mass and to regulate bodily functions. We know that individuals require different foods and process them differently. We want to study the effects of diet on each student. In the schools we license, we will suggest they have most dietary requests available—gluten-free, vegan, vegetarian, paleo, for example—and that they use software to monitor the students' attention throughout their educational experiences each day. Switching to a different diet to further test academic impact or lack of impact would be fully voluntary, but the students would be exposed to documentaries and academic materials regarding nutrition and the impact on brain function to back up the tests.

Schools using our free license in the test stage will offer a much-needed laboratory to try out these ideas.

The actual information available about the proper diet for learning is full of noise. It's unreliable. Since the brain is a huge consumer of energy, some believe that high carbohydrates are needed. Others believe that high protein is required, because of the crash in energy a few hours after carbohydrates are consumed. By giving the kids breakfast and lunch we can finally solve the problem for each individual student, since our software recognizes the moment of cognition and can then identify the conditions that preceded understanding. What was in the last meal, and how long ago was it? Did the student have any snacks or stimulants such as coffee or cola?

Kids who want to opt in to the tests will follow a strict diet both at school—where they'd eat only the nutrient balances we are studying—and at home. (We would be sending the meals home for the student and, if we are able to secure funding, for the family.) We believe that we can increase student outcomes by answering the diet questions precisely and matching the diet to the student's DNA. Students who joined the test would be able to earn extra $Eds.[8]

This is an ideal opportunity to give the students who participate in the study academic peer-reviewed, published backup material. We could show documentaries with credible sources and citations about food and sleep and also supply audiobooks and reading material that would be helpful in establishing a base understanding of the core issues around what we eat and how we relate to the world.

Kids are always hungry; their high metabolism requires calories often. We would offer healthy protein and carbohydrate options for between-meal snackers. The idea is to supply nutrition without the empty calories and make it easily accessible.

continued

---

8   An $Ed is much like a token or ticket in a Chuck E. Cheese. Students will be able to use them for digital purchases of time and freedoms. There will be enough desirable purchase possibilities that gaining more $Eds will be a motivating factor in helping the students take agency over their education.

We will encourage good habits, but we will not prejudge. If a kid needs a 300-calorie boost, a candy bar may be just the thing. We hope that if highly nutritious options are available, the student will reach for one of those as they see a connection to a better mood and educational outcome.

High school students use more stimulants these days than 20 years ago. Coffee, green tea, and black tea are all part of the current teens' diet, and we will study them as well. Having tea or coffee available for consumption in the cubicles will offer a research-rich environment.

The combination of exercise and diet should make our students the most physically healthy and alert in the nation. This approach—and our hypothesis—will benefit from the ability to research the impact of nutrition and sleep on students' learning. We will also research the effect on our students' ability to overcome obstacles and face challenges. It would be hard to imagine obesity taking hold if a child were fully engaged in this program.

NASA has done many studies regarding how much sleep and when to sleep for the best outcomes. A 20-minute nap after lunch could make the afternoon more productive for a student. Learning when rested works. It is a staple for kindergarten. Many European and Spanish-speaking countries include naps as part of their culture. Our schools will provide the time and the place for kids to take naps in a quiet and darkened space. The students could sign up for a particular time and receive reminders when the time expires. $Eds can be used to take a nap at other times, say when a student has been up the previous night till three in the morning playing video games. It would seem more productive to give the student extra sleep than to have a dull brain working on a lesson. A lecture about getting to bed earlier has not worked for generations. A nap can help solve plenty of problems.

Schools could operate the kitchen as well as the nap room in shifts. The reality of feeding and sleeping 300-plus kids requires planning and a schedule. We will need supervision in these darkened spaces, but we believe the benefits will be worth the expense and the problems that could arise.

Sleep is important to learning, and getting enough sleep is key to enhanced outcomes. In some of our schools we plan to have weekday sleepovers. If the students are fed two meals a day, the cost of adding another meal and supervision for overnight stays in the nap rooms represent a small additional cost and can ensure that students get plenty of rest. Mandatory lights out also removes the stimulation of video games and TV.

ACCOMMODATE EACH STUDENT'S HOME LIFE

A Monday-to-Friday sleepover school for inner cities could help address multiple problems and offer interested students and families a sense of security surrounding education. In Nolan's proposal the kids stay at school from Monday morning until Friday afternoon, and with the library and internet available there, the students would have no weekend homework. That schedule also eliminates the problem many young inner-city students experience walking to and from school with a book bag that could contain valuable technology.

So many parents in these inner-city areas work two and three jobs to keep food on the table and a roof over their heads. They are often exhausted when they come home, and then the children are their next job before they can sleep. If they knew the children were safe and learning from Monday to Friday, the weekend experience with the child might be richer and more enjoyable for both the children and the parents. The lack of homework on the weekend means quality family time or simply that time to slow down and pursue personal interests like sports or music is more available.

For five days every week the child has nothing to worry about. After-school sports, games, social life, and educational support are all on tap. Graduate students in education could be hired as support staff to teachers and mentors to students. With some university involvement, the grad students could also be earning credit toward their MA in education.

HEALTHY AT HOME

Another thing we've learned from the 2020 pandemic is that we make decisions every day that impact our longevity. COVID-19 attacked those who were struggling with problems like diabetes, asthma, or obesity. The virus seems to thrive in a body that is fighting health issues of varying degrees. That may be one of the reasons that the United States has had such high numbers of deaths from the virus. We are likely to see research in the near future that addresses the overall health issues in our country, compared to Italy, China, and other countries that dealt with the virus and managed to control enough to let people return to their normal lives.

We all need to take charge of what we can do to keep ourselves safe, and that goes beyond a mask, social distancing, and washing your hands. It requires that we become a healthier nation.

Every time we lift a fork to our mouth, we are making decisions that will determine our vulnerability to disease. Having a program in schools that encourages healthy eating habits and better sleep could offer a rich environment to nurture a healthy generation.

We need to take sleep seriously. My daughter is a fifth-grade teacher, and she can, within a few days of the beginning of the school year, tell what a child's sleep habits are. Her school has brought in experts to speak with parents about the importance of sleep for their children's education. Nevertheless my granddaughter shows me text messages from her sixth-grade peers that were sent at midnight and two a.m.

The Way We're Working Isn't Working by Tony Schwartz addresses this issue through his own and others' research into the impact of sleep on athletes, students, and executives. Schwartz also busts the myth of "effective multitasking," which he and other experts consider an oxymoron for most adults. It will be interesting to see if this will still be true when those who are currently completing early elementary school are adults.

Kids today are on the computer with the TV on and their friends on the iPad next to the computer while they request favorite songs from their smart speaker. Will they be better at multitasking as a result of this ability to split their focus? This is a question in need of study. Again, Nolan's school program will offer a rich source of new research on effective educational methods.

It would take a rather ill-informed educator or parent to argue against the need for serious consideration of nutrition and sleep.

PRINCIPLE #4.
OPTIMIZE BRAIN ACTIVITY, NEUROGENESIS, AND MENTAL PLASTICITY

In the same way that weight lifting makes muscles stronger, critical thinking makes the brain stronger. The brain is capable of growing and responding to exercises not only of the mind but also of the body. Mind and body are so linked in a dance of chemicals and responses that it is almost impossible to talk about the mind without talking about health, exercise, and diet. The big thing to realize is that rigorous exercise followed by learning modules—learning of any type, really—can make anyone smarter. Yes, anyone can raise their IQ by several points by applying what we know about nutrition and neuroscience. The skeptics will say that people are simply learning how to take IQ tests, but it is more than that. Cognitive thinking and problem-solving become enhanced as a result of practice.

To optimize brain activity, neurogenesis, and mental plasticity, we encourage physical movement. Movement is essential, because it's also fun and engaging and helps the kids bond with each other. You can start the day with dancing, basketball, running, or exercise classes, to name a few choices. The activity a student chooses is important only for the individual. The key is that they are moving. Empirical evidence shows the importance of physical activity on brain development beyond infancy and early childhood. It's hard to stay sad while dancing or running.

Most peer-reviewed research has been conducted on rewiring the brain after injury or trauma, yet we believe the findings inform brain development beyond injuries. The hypothesis is that you can maintain neuroplasticity through rigorous physical activity while you also create habits that will support that development, habits like attention to nutrition and the development of effective sleep practices.

I've already mentioned John Medina's *Brain Rules*. I highly recommend it. He has conducted and compiled research to present a compelling picture of how the brain works. Medina confirms Tony Schwartz's declaration that multitasking is a myth. The two writers complement each other: Medina's focus is on what sleep and stress do to our brain's ability to absorb new information; Schwartz presents research on the effects of sleep on our brain.

Abraham Maslow first published his hierarchy of needs in 1943 to a skeptical psychological society. However, most recent research regarding brain development and elasticity confirms his suspicions that we are not capable of realizing our full potential or being open to new information when we are focused on basic needs like food, shelter, or safety.

This research is important to the discussions about education reform. According to Maslow, Medina, and Schwartz, we could have a significant impact on the future of our culture by making sure that exercise, nutrition, and sleep habits are well established by middle school and then reinforced throughout middle and high school years.

In *Spark: The Revolutionary New Science of Exercise and the Brain*, John J. Ratey outlines his research on learning and mood as a result of exercise. He has identified a whole series of benefits of exercise as a solution for many classroom ailments such as hostility, ADHD, anxiety, PMS, and depression, as well as just learning better and faster with better recall. The key

continued

is to exercise vigorously for at least 20 minutes at 80 percent of your maximum heart rate quotient. (Your maximum heart rate is found by subtracting age from 220. So a kid of 10 has a theoretical maximum of 210 and should exercise at 168 beats per minute.)

Ratey believes that soon everyone will be talking about neurogenesis and the building of brain matter. When someone exercises aggressively for 20 minutes, the brain secretes BDNF or brain-derived neurotrophic factor. Ratey calls this "Miracle-Gro for the brain." It is part of the axon or dendrites protein complex and appears to put newly learned thoughts into totally new pathways. Exercise this way often, and the brain gets more complex and heavy, more flexible and able to withstand dementia and Alzheimer's.

Even mild exercise such as walking or stretching is beneficial to the learner, and if the exercise is associated with learning a skill, the positive effect on the brain is even greater. For example, ballroom dancing, yoga, martial arts, tai chi, skiing, snowboarding, and even skateboarding are all skills that build brain function and require physical exercise. We will create several special games that require physical exercise to play; the games will monitor the exertion and pace the curriculum to the desired level of exercise.

Many children have too much energy to sit still in a classroom; some of them may actually be self-medicating by fidgeting or tapping their feet. They learn better and stay focused better with a slightly elevated heart rate.

What do these findings mean for school? Ideally it will have two exercise periods of 20 minutes—one before school and one about an hour after lunch.

As Nolan points out, some people simply think better when they move. Adults pace when trying to think through a problem. Kids fidget. A school should adapt to these learning and thinking patterns. We could have both treadmill desks and activity games that can be used to elevate heart rate while students work on portions of modules. While learning difficult material, it may be effective for the student to engage in vigorous exercise, and even milder movement such as walking or leisurely pedaling a bike could be helpful. Movement like this may be required for some to achieve maximum effective learning. The integration of exercise into learning may be the most important step of all to increase brain activity, neurogenesis, and mental plasticity.

PRINCIPLE #5.
USE SMALL GROUPS TO PROVIDE DEEPER UNDERSTANDING OF SUBJECTS

Group study puts concepts into context. And groups challenge our understanding of the world by pushing back on our standards and our ideas. They challenge our philosophy. Finding others who have the same questions and beliefs is an important part of learning, but so is the ability to hear ideas different from our own and find common ground.

continued

Teachers can keep the conversation focused on the subject at hand, or they can encourage a group to range more widely. The end goal of the group experience, beyond the curriculum, is the time spent exploring each other's ideas. There are many opportunities for group discussion; keeping the groups small can bring the quieter voices to the discussion.

The discussions we envision are not confined to the discussion rooms. Group projects, building a larger project, making a movie, or solving a business problem all offer opportunities for group meetings. These are all dynamic situations that impart skills and understanding of group dynamics and help students hone their skills to debate, adjust ideas based on new facts, and develop their voice as an advocate for oneself. Interactivity is the key, and small groups offer little chance for someone to hide. The small groups can then report out to the larger community, giving the chance for the more gregarious students to experience the charge of presenting to the crowd.

Public speaking is difficult for most people and can only become easy with practice. Speaking to small groups on a regular basis is the first step toward building that presentation muscle. Debate and mock government can give additional chances for a student to speak and deliver ideas to a group. Delivering a speech with a PowerPoint presentation is a skill everyone needs. Product pitches designed to raise money, promote a project, or simply talk to a club or group will help build the confidence and routine of public speaking. These are skills that every high school kid should have.

Making movies or YouTube videos is another way to encourage kids to be comfortable performing in public. Having kids give a lesson to younger kids is also beneficial for both the presenter and the listener. Often the best way to learn is to teach.

Politics and history are great subjects for discussion groups because they are as much about belief as about the data underlying those beliefs. They offer an opportunity to examine how we feel about the way the world operates. In order for those conversations to be productive, however, we need students who can think critically, listen to different perspectives, and make decisions and adjustments in their own theories based on evidence and convincing arguments.

Group discussions are an effective method of engaging a classroom of students. Too often, quieter students will simply listen. Though they may have ideas to share, they'll keep those to themselves. Larger group discussions introduce the risk of ridicule and embarrassment and often create anxiety for quieter students. Breaking into smaller work groups and assigning a few questions that everyone needs to address can get the quieter students engaged and allow for a deeper dive into areas of concentration.

There is plenty of evidence that peer-to-peer learning is effective, which further underscores the importance of small-group sessions. Antioch University Los Angeles professor Dr. Albert Erdynast uses this small-group practice and has for more than 40 years. He has found it to be helpful in multiple ways. Why should we wait until a student is in higher education to use this all the time rather than as the exception to the rule of lecture-based classrooms?

Students often take the time to inform each other of their personal experiences with a given topic, which demonstrates their own vulnerability and in turn invites openness and vulnerability from the listener and others in the group. In time, even shyer students may become more comfortable sharing their opinions beyond the small group. The quiet students may hear their ideas shared by a classmate in a larger group setting, with that classmate crediting them for finding the information. Dr. Erdynast notes that hearing their ideas shared by other students can make quieter students less intimidated in the future.

The chance to understand and be understood is inherent in small-group discussions. Students have a chance to take their time in opening up about ideas in challenging areas. At its best, education encourages such challenges. That's where our most profound learning and evolution takes place. Finding your way through those challenges is where the rewards are.

Seldom do we hear a success story that recounts an easy path from start to finish. Growth happens when our world blows up a lot or a little. Challenges propel us to be better, smarter, and kinder, or we can dig into our anger and frustration and hold tight to where we were when the problem presented itself. Our role as educators is to help a child evaluate the learning and help them ask better questions so they land on the side of progress. The input of classmates in these small-group settings can be valuable confirmation.

Socratic discussion is beneficial for many subjects, but, again, interactivity is the key. Kids in small groups can all be participants. Small discussion rooms with 8 to 12 students—either led by a teacher or self-led—make these interactions productive for all. Having 35 students in a classroom does not allow interactivity. The extroverts take over the conversation, and the introverts offer their thoughts to no one.

Volumes have been written, and hours of debate and discussion have been endured by curious members of the community engaged in the conversation around school reform. Making room for small-group discussions in the physical space as well as the pedagogy would be a good starting point.

CHAPTER 6

Cultivate Enthusiasm and Creativity

PRINCIPLE #6.
LEARNING BY DOING WITH
TOOLS AND INSTRUMENTS

Tool use is neurogenic; the very use of tools help build brain connectivity. Hands-on projects teach skills in a broad spectrum of subjects. Many projects require math, physics, chemistry, and history. With tools and scientific instruments available, a student can acquire a broad set of skills. This does not mean just prototyping, it is also about using a green screen, video cameras, and both audio and video editing. It is about planting and caring for plants in a greenhouse and garden plot. Instruments are fun and empowering, and a wide variety of scientific instruments can bring almost anything into sharper focus.

continued

A very-high-power video microscope can bring the world of the tiny into view for exploration and examination. Often the world of the tiny is beautiful and can be the foundation of an art piece. Images of skin cells or butterfly wings can be simply and easily added to projects, for example. In order to explore these areas, however, the students need easy access to tools.

Being part of creating a movie can be fun and rewarding. Acting is one way to treat shyness, while writing and directing are important life skills in a YouTube world. To be the star in a YouTube short is fun for the actor as well as their parents and grandparents. Not everyone needs to be the star, though. Passion and enthusiasm can come from being part of a scene, making costumes, building sets, directing lighting, providing the original music, or focusing on proper sound effects. These all fit into the realm of exploring through the arts. So often in life we feel the need to be all things and berate ourselves when we lack a talent for something we are about to embark on. Working on a production is a real-world example of applying each person's strengths to complete the project.

Music is more than something extra on a school curriculum. It's the center of a full education, linked not only to mathematics but also to personal passions.

Musical instruments are accessible, cheap, and powerful. Keyboards that can be plugged into the cubicle computer with a USB can give rise to powerful learning software and, even more interesting, music editing. In this way writing and playing music become part of the curriculum.

Learning to play electric guitar is similarly easy with software, and listening through headphones enables many students to practice at the same time in their cubicles. Other instruments can be practiced in a few soundproof rooms or on a sound stage. Even electronic drum sets will make little noise unless you turn on the amplifier.

Making art is always creative. Ceramics, painting with oil or watercolors, or using the hottest computer graphics programs are all part of the creative process. Building artworks with lights and microprocessors that are sound or light activated brings out technical as well as artistic skills. A 3-D printer is an easy way to take a design and make a physical object. Mathematics often underpin wild and wonderful designs. A large percentage of kids today have an idea for a video game. Let that be a driver for their passion and also for learning, since video games require not only a great deal of creativity but also many skills.

Cooking and clothing design are also outlets for experimentation and creation, and both can be the foundation of a wonderful career.

Nolan is making a strong point for engagement. Learning by doing is becoming a rallying cry of educators. More than a lecture, a project that requires research on a topic and final submission—a paper or a deck outlining the problem and the competing claims around the central issue, for example—can engage the student at a deep and meaningful level. A student will recall more about a project shared by another student than anything conveyed by an adult lecturing at the front of the room.

The student could prototype their inventions and then build an argument and propose a solution explaining what their invention answers. They can share their reactions and conclusions based on what they have studied and what they have devised as a solution. It is hard to argue with information you find yourself. We have countless examples of people who are who they are because that is the way their family has always been, or that is the way their parents, school, teachers—whoever the voice of authority is in their subconscious—led them. Having access to tools and the space to explore a subject and draw conclusions about the subject and their inventions allow for exploration of new fields and access to new career considerations.

If a young person finds answers based on experimentation and facts from credible sources, they may adjust their understanding of a subject based on new information. However, without the desire or ability to research their ideas, they are likely to reject new information that doesn't fit their worldview. Students will be at different stages of this experience throughout middle and high school. It benefits all of us if they use this time to build their worldview based on peer-reviewed, culturally respectful articles and research. Learning by doing incorporates learning by what others have been doing. And that requires research.

TEACH THE ABILITY TO THRIVE

Listen to a few minutes of the news, and we can all find a dozen reasons to feel bleak. The truth is, there are always problems. Building a student's muscle for enthusiasm, optimism, and passion may be the only way to not only survive but to thrive in difficult times.

PRINCIPLE #7.
OFFER PROGRAMS THAT INSPIRE LIFE SKILLS
OF ENTHUSIASM, OPTIMISM, AND PASSION

No one goes through this life without struggles. Learning to meet them head-on with an attitude that says, "We can do this" will make for a much more pleasant experience in the midst of struggle than reacting with fear, anger, or denial. Failure is an important part of the experience. Failure is a stepping-stone to new information, not evidence that we are a failure. That doesn't mean that we don't feel the pain and disappointment of failure in the moment. It just means we don't stay with that feeling. We move quickly to evaluate the situation and create a game plan for addressing it. We go back to the start and brainstorm ideas for the next version, helped ideally by the attention of a thoughtful and patient educator.

When challenged at just the right level of difficulty, a student breezes through the matter and enters the state of flow, the complete harmony of interest and progress identified by psychologist Mihaly Csikszentmihalyi in his book *Flow*. I believe that by adopting Csikszentmihalyi's methods, the enthusiasm for learning, students' natural curiosity, and applied creativity could all be nurtured and kept vibrant. Which is of course the natural state of every young child. Csikszentmihalyi puts forth the idea that finding your flow informs a lifelong love of learning. When we design video games, we attempt to keep players in flow as much as possible.

Csikszentmihalyi's book was on the reading list in graduate school, and it was one of those books that your reason and your intuition told you was full of meaningful information.

As Nolan points out, the evidence is clear that the video game industry has been effective at keeping kids in that state of flow while they play; it makes them want to stay in the game. A much broader conversation is needed here regarding students who are labeled with attention deficit disorder. Nolan insists that those students have no problem focusing in a video game but have a terrible time doing that in class. Perhaps we need to acknowledge that in many of these cases the student isn't engaged because we have not engaged them with education that inspires learning. That needs to be considered in the approach of all schools interested in competing with the temptations in front of the child.

> The goal is to create a program that has students so engaged in their education, and optimistic about their abilities and their ability to learn, that they understand that with effort and dedication there are no limits to their future careers and life in general.
>
> Our modules will follow all state-mandated curriculums but will do it in a way that the student doesn't feel burdened.

The idea of hiding testing in games and platforms the student is already interested in has merit. Student engagement is key, and we need data to measure how best to do that. If test preparation can be added to a playful experience like a video game, we can begin to collect that important data. It is often access to students and the need for tools to measure their progress that hinders effective real-time research in education. As mentioned earlier, there are plenty of games being designed by academics. The children are rarely fooled by them. They see these as education delivered as a game. What we need is for the game to be the draw and the education to be a natural result of engagement in the game. For that, we need game designers. The academic community can identify what needs to be covered, and the game designers can make it happen in a way that engages the students.

Ultimately, how our kids score on standardized tests will be the cornerstone on which we prove or disprove the effectiveness of our theory. We think standardized tests delivered in games would avoid the anxiety many students feel when they know they are taking a test.

We also believe our graduates will be sought by the best universities and the most desirable employers. In the end, that will be the best evidence for our approach to education.

While standardized exams do not test enthusiasm, optimism, or creativity, these tests would be necessary to prove the power of this type of education to the academic community at large; how the tests are given is up for consideration. Building the requisite tests into an experience that the student is already engaged with and comfortable in could offer valuable insight.

DISCOVER STUDENTS' HIDDEN TALENTS

The school of the future's software modules provide a series of pleasant new ideas to the student that slowly build understanding and enthusiasm for their education. The software also has thousands of data points that can quickly make statistical comparisons and help discover a student's hidden talents. Everyone wants to become talented. Not everyone wants to put in the time or effort to excel. We expect that this new version of education will help find the student's undiscovered abilities and help them maximize their individual potential.

Listening to a child and gauging their enthusiasm is key to identifying the interests that can help hone the student's talent. Again, for a teacher with a room full of students, it is hard to find the time to work with each individual and understand their interests. Not all children will easily open up about their dreams to an adult, even when the adult is a teacher they like.

The data points Nolan mentions offer a quick fix for that part of the challenge. Once we know a child's interests, it is easier to engage them in work that explores those interests. This isn't to say that we should only introduce subjects that are already of interest to the student; it is simply the starting point of engaging them in their academic life. For example, if we know a student is crazy about music, we could ask them to write about their favorite musician. We are then engaging them in research and helping to develop their writing skills.

From there we can ask about the family life of the musician. Where did they grow up? Who were their parents? Where did their ancestors come from? What was the political environment at the time? Did they tour? Can you create a map of the tour? The educator's job is not to answer these questions but to help come up with them. If you leave some space in the conversation with the student, you find out what the student is already curious about. Those are the best questions, even if they are not well thought out or elaborate, because these questions are evidence of curiosity. And, above all, we want to promote curiosity, which will inform the students' life well beyond school.

We know from years of research that there are many different natural abilities and intelligences. Howard Gardner, a developmental psychologist at Harvard, has spent his life understanding the facets of these different intelligences. We have spent years applying them to our software so that it will engage the students. Video games have created a large body of knowledge about engagement, rewards, and passion. Let's use that to the advantage of the young learner. Many games are difficult yet manage to engage children to the level of addiction. We will use all this understanding and, by applying emerging data on brain science, continually improve our outcomes.

We are just at the starting line of the revolution in education, but if we want to make a difference, we are going to need to adapt some of what we have learned about engagement in video games to education. Gardner has published many papers regarding differences in learning. Using these insights from success in video games would change the dynamic in the student's level of commitment. The video game industry has already been using them to the advantage of the game, effectively keeping kids engaged. But education has for the most part ignored

Gardner's work when planning curriculum, school days, and the delivery methods for education. The idea that we could develop a learning system that applies all that we know about learning habits and is exciting to educators and any parent who has experienced a student with different learning abilities.

> The future can be exciting when you consider all that can be accomplished if children are fully engaged and feel recognized for their differences and their need for an effective education.

This is the most promising part of Nolan's proposed ideas for education. Applying what the video games have been learning, testing, and developing as a result of their interest and exposure to brain research will likely be the most impactful. The hardest thing to change is an attitude. Especially an attitude that has developed without any thought for why. Teachers are likely to be the first to accept this approach. The administration and departments of education nationwide may be the hardest to reach. Accepted attitudes about how to educate students is often backed, promoted (with deep pockets), and lobbied for by the textbook industry.

Valerie Strauss of the *Washington Post* reported in 2015 on the millions of dollars spent by Pearson Education, Houghton Mifflin Harcourt, Educational Testing Service, and McGraw-Hill as they lobbied to promote testing in America. The reason is obvious when you consider that testing is a $2 billion annual business. Not surprisingly, many civil servants in education departments in state and federal offices find lucrative jobs at those publishing companies when they leave civil service.

None of that would be a problem if the student were the focus of the effort. But I'm not convinced that the emphasis is on students first. If it were, we would be considering the weight of the physical books as well as the need to make the curriculum more enjoyable and engaging.

Significant research exists regarding learning and testing, but it is mostly absent when developing current curriculum. There are exceptions, including the earlier mentioned *Brain Rules* by John Medina, and *Invent to Learn* by Sylvia Libow Martinez and Gary Stager, PhD. These authors and many others have books and research that can both inspire and inform those conversations.

There's no need to invent a new system of thinking about education. We simply have to engage with these progressive thinkers and bring the best practices they promote into the student's experience. Nolan's proposed system of educating moved to the top of my list when we began talking about student needs and engagement. He is also finding the best teachers to develop modules to work with the best in game design. The end result should be myriad games that address curriculum needs and support optimism, enthusiasm, and passion.

We will integrate some of the effective techniques used in the development of video games. Most of the top-tier gaming companies have child psychologists on staff making recommendations for how to engage the child. There are some interesting games that allow a student to project life paths, which can be an integrated way of instilling optimism. These methods being used in games can also be applied to education. Then we can test for academic progress along with measuring enthusiasm and optimism levels in students. That will allow us to quickly determine what is working and what is not working with each student. It will also offer new methods of testing inside games that will lower the anxiety levels in the student.

Enthusiasm is contagious. If enthusiastic kids are around troubled kids, some of the enthusiasm may rub off. Having

continued

a broad variety of things that engender optimism also helps keep the level of enthusiasm high. With individualized learning it is easier to determine what might be a stretch and what might be an easy win for a student in need of encouragement.

Ultimately, enthusiasm for one subject or project can spill over into other pursuits, and we will be actively pursuing ways to ensure this can happen. Having various ways of engaging students will help us learn what keeps them engaged beyond the must-do portion of the subject. What makes them come back to learn more? What are they still thinking about a few hours later?

Our retired-professional volunteer system also allows kids to have cost-effective professional help beyond the curriculum when needed. There are many retired psychologists or faith-based leaders who would be willing and able to spend time helping a student, conceptualizing an approach or educational road map for the student, and creating a plan with a follow-up schedule. The idea is to make this mentoring program simple to access and to encourage the students to deal with problems as they arise, before they become lifelong issues.

Parents and the home environment can be a huge asset or can create extreme handicaps for learning. The most predictive factor of good outcomes is a stable household. If parents are constantly fighting or are going through a divorce, the kids almost always suffer. Difficult situations also arise where the parents have to work multiple jobs, and the student is alone more than is desirable. Sometimes counseling a student's parents will be the best way to help a child thrive.

This is part of the logic for our plan to add a Monday-to-Friday boarding option for inner-city schools. If students are heavily stressed from their environment, it can be a challenge for the best of educational intentions. Simply staying at school from Monday to Friday can reduce stress on parents and give kids a chance to excel. The rich mentoring and educational environment will be important, while sleeping arrangements and food can be surprisingly low cost. Having a facility where kids learn how to do laundry and take care of themselves during those Monday-to-Friday stays will also help develop good life skills.

The kids will have regular health checkups on campus. This will help us track any virus, but it is also an easy way to tell if kids are stressed. There are scientific tests that will give us an idea of stress levels and indicate the success or failure of our interventions. If the kids are stressed, it will be on us to try to mitigate whatever is causing the problem.

Optimism and enthusiasm are the precursors to passion. There are hundreds of self-help books that purport to help in these areas and a significant amount of research on ways to keep students happy and enthusiastic. Exercise will cause a generally more positive outlook, but there are several other ideas we will employ. Neurolinguistic programming is full of physical exercises that have proven to work. We would integrate these exercises into the school.

We would also start each day with a series of images and words that are positive and invigorating and ask the students to repeat them out loud. We will tell the kids the benefit of this

continued

activity, and, though some will scoff at the practice, enough will give it a try so that we can test their attitude in double-blind tests to find efficacy.

Searching for beauty is another way of escaping the mundane and imagining a better world and environment. Virtual tours of mountains, rivers, or grasslands, or showing artworks can put a person into a different and more positive state. There are a host of other exercises that have worked in the game industry that are worthy of consideration in education. Those that work will be kept and enhanced. The self-help community is full of wonderful ideas, some theoretical, others tested. We will measure these as we search for solutions for each student and create individualized learning programs.

We believe that we can find passion in every child. Our hypothesis is that the passion for one subject can be converted into ambition and drive in other disciplines and in life in general. Since we will be starting our system with kids at 13 years old, we expect there will be many unmotivated kids. Much of the enthusiasm children have in first grade has been somewhat damaged by middle school. Still, some will be okay and will have developed coping mechanisms with a sense of curiosity and adventure.

We know that many kids, particularly boys, have a passion for video games. We can show any 13-year-old without computer skills how a game level is created in less than an hour. They can add physical elements like trees to a game within minutes. They can then play the level they just designed.

Creating games that will interest other students is often a way to get kids interested in understanding math and engineering. Each success opens the pathway to passion.

At the Bushnell house, my children were always creating and designing games and experiences. They all knew that the way to engage Dad was to start a project. As adults, they do much the same. Those early experiences of invention and trial and error have informed their career paths.

Parents don't need to be an expert or even mildly knowledgeable about the subjects they expose their kids to; they simply need to allow room for the child to try and fail and try again. That's how kids build confidence. There are occasions when we just need to make sure there are a few easy wins in a child's education to help them build self-assurance. Then we can eventually introduce more difficult challenges.

CULTIVATE CREATIVITY
THROUGH GAME DESIGN

Game design can become addictive to kids. Showing friends and family the game they have developed and watching them play the game will build confidence and deepen their desire to continue. Once kids have figured out how to place trees, rocks, and terrain in their game design, they'll want whatever is next.

continued

It may be that they want to learn about walls and colors and lighting and computer-generated players. Each of these steps is a little harder, and some require changing a "script," which involves first-level programming but at an understandable level. By the time the game design gets difficult, the students are invested in the progress and curious about what might be at the next level. It becomes an easy introduction to a whole series of skills in different disciplines.

Math and engineering become interesting, as they inform the complexity of the games students can develop. The students will need to communicate both to players and to others in the game-design world to gain access to more difficult skill sets. The importance of communicating is true for everything from school to career, and being a good communicator will be an asset throughout life. In this case the task is to communicate a message as a game designer.

Not everyone will attend a four-year university. There are plenty of rewarding jobs that are skill based. Cabinetmakers, builders, farmers—these are all career choices that don't require higher education. Being a good communicator, however, will help regardless of the level of education or career choice.

Digital literacy is also important. Tools for graphics like Photoshop or 3-D authoring tools all help build desirable skills and will help draw many students to campus. Just learning one of these programs to moderate proficiency will provide an occupation that is nearly always in short supply. People who have experience with Maya, Lightwave, or 3D Studio Max for digital movie effects, animated features, games, or advertising command starting salaries over $100,000 per year.

With passion, learning skills can be fun and challenging at the same time. Nolan's suggestion that not all kids will want or need a four-year degree was hard for me to hear as a passionate educator. I want all students to have access to higher education, but I understand his point that not everyone will need or want that access. When students follow a passion, they learn what they need to, and that doesn't always have to be delivered in a formal educational setting. Perhaps students working on a project find that they need some math as they increase their skills, or they may need to understand physics.

I was recently speaking with two brothers, Connor and Bauer Lee, who have been building life-size superheroes out of cardboard since elementary school. They told me of the trial and errors in the first few builds and what they learned about ratios, physics, and math in general as they perfected their statues.

Learning math to solve a problem in your project is quite different from learning math in a row of kids being lectured to from a teacher. The Lee brothers have no trouble recalling what they've learned and how they learned it in service of their end result. I, on the other hand, can tell you nothing of any math lecture from elementary through high school. These brothers, who are now in high school, are evidence of the theory that learning by doing is real and it lasts.

We also need the ability to create narrative for games and because of that, sentence structure becomes important. Character creation also needs costume design, and dressing the character brings out the need for fashion sense. Often a time period is important so the student's interest in history is piqued. All games have some rules about money and value, therefore some economic understanding would be helpful. Instead of learning by lecture, the student seeks information that will help them fulfill their game or project or interest. All of this requires research.

Games provide a context for learning. The creation of an artificial world prompts serious questions about the world we are in. Isn't learning how the world works one of the goals of education? This concept is rich with possibility. Older students making games to help younger students learn helps on several levels. The older student recalls what was required of them when they were in the younger grades, anchoring their learning. Younger students give feedback to the older student about the design, what works, and what doesn't. The older student learns about designing for a constituent while also learning to take critical feedback and apply the feedback to the design. The younger student learns to articulate their thoughts and ideas in reaction to something. These are skills that will be beneficial throughout life.

Another way passion can be kindled is through eBay. Some kids have natural marketing and sales abilities. They have been marketed to all their life and have been saturated by sales pitches in the media. Turning the tables and giving them a platform to sell can be a natural experience for them. By allowing kids to set up accounts and sell stuff, we will help them develop valuable life skills and a sense of letting things go when they have served a purpose, and in the process they supply themselves a source of income.

The maker movement can also be a passion builder. Tool use and a culture of making things leads to these questions: Can these things I am making be sold? Can these things I'm using be made, or made better? If we extend the school day earlier and later—to 8 to 5—there will be at least four hours available for passion-driven projects. This could be anything from making, selling, practicing, dancing, painting, programming, or designing, basically having a good time with a rich environment of things, ideas, and images.

Passion for anything can be a great driver for academics. We will design the system so that it requires a certain amount of academic modules be completed to open up resources for passion projects.

Increasingly we hear that top chefs started at an early age with a passion for cooking, and it has become clear to all who had access to the end product that they could do it with style even as youngsters. Our kitchen will be available for those with creative culinary ambitions, particularly if that inspires a child's passion.

I remember a great conversation I had one night in Paris after a fabulous meal with the late three-star chief Alain Senderens. It was about all things chemistry. He talked about how he tests the pH of many of his ingredients as a precursor to his preparation and said that the blending of ingredients was nothing more than creating the right chemical reactions. I was fascinated and somewhat surprised.

In any student population, there are students who are extraordinary. Some students are smart and driven, and others are less motivated and difficult to engage. This latter group may move into the former group if they feel heard and their interests are encouraged and honored. Some students are slow

continued

to grasp and remember the subject matter. On this platform, that is fine as long as they are engaged and moving in the direction of gathering knowledge and/or skills. In contrast, the current classroom is a horror for many students. Forcing a student to go down the hall to the classroom for special needs or tutoring can be horrible for a kid who is trying to fit in.

The software delivery of educational material on a personalized basis allows all kids to look alike and does not single out anyone for ridicule for being slow or fast. There are school cultures that make it "not cool" to be good at school; being a stealth scholar is now possible. The worst thing that can happen is for a student to be placed in a classroom in which the subject is over their head. The only thing the student can do then is tune out or become disruptive.

Our job and goal as educators is to engage the child and inspire them to learn. So much of what Nolan describes here makes that job more fulfilling for teachers and accessible to students. The idea that if we expose students to enough areas of potential engagement then they could be inspired to learn what they need to know to excel once they find an interest. Given an environment that builds confidence—and offers challenges that are possible wins for the student—they can open doors that might have previously appeared impossible to unlock.

CHAPTER 7

Target Individual Interests and Schedules

PRINCIPLE #8.
CREATE AN ENVIRONMENT THAT CAN ENCOURAGE EVERYONE TO THRIVE

In order to thrive regardless of talent, it is important to have the ability to communicate. One of the biggest complaints about high school graduates and even college graduates is the poor quality of their writing. We believe that the adaptive practice and game methods of the school of the future can be applied to make kids write often and well.

Our solution is to create the need for frequent quick-response writing inside the game. Many times kids overthink compositions when they really just need to write something to get in the practice of seeing and evaluating their work.

continued

Reading is also an important component in developing as a writer. Experiencing how others make their points and tell stories encourages the reader to think about how they might approach this subject or another based on what they are reading.

The amount of writing will be commensurate with a student's ability and where they are in their studies. For example, six-year-old students could write a sentence to describe their interests while a 15-year-old will write a couple of pages. In four to five years we would have measurable data from the program indicating the effectiveness of language arts development. The impact on the students' writing ability would inform the development of the next level of gamified curriculum.

Languages will be offered and encouraged, as well as trades and manual skills. A student's interest will dictate their study paths. Being multilingual brings a host of benefits and can propel a career in one direction, while other students' interests and expertise in trades and manual skills will open different doors. The goal is to allow students to get credit for having a wide range of knowledge about a variety of subjects and then to help them drill down into the areas in which they are most interested.

Following interests allows for the students' abilities to lead the exploration, which will help the students apply creative and critical thinking as well as problem-solving. It also drives many other skills that need to be developed to write effectively. Research, documenting your research, writing your reports, and offering your ideas all work toward establishing your interest and your place in the study of that interest.

The earlier example of the Lee brothers helps make this point. The boys both are top of their class in math. This didn't happen because they loved the homework, it happened because they had issues they needed to address with the superheroes they were creating, and math and physics offered those solutions.

Understanding challenges in one discipline can benefit from the examination of problems in another discipline. That cross-cultural understanding applied to a new problem can be where the most productive answers are found.

Malcolm Gladwell, in his book *Outliers*, talks about the need for 10,000 hours of practice to become elite in a sport or music.[9] This is a principle easily applied to a variety of endeavors. A large amount of time spent on something of interest develops that muscle. Unfortunately, this doesn't happen in our educational system. If we give the students agency over their education and offer them the opportunity to dive into their interests we may see those 10,000 hours completed at young ages. It might feel okay for a student to acknowledge that they may not be good at something if they know they are good at something else. Discovering what they are good at is not often a short-term project.

We take the number of hours seriously in all disciplines and find it particularly helpful when it comes to writing. Reading rich material helps with writing but, mostly, writing helps with writing. If the kids start writing age-appropriate sentences and paragraphs every day, they will become good communicators. Some will become authors and poets, but all of them will use their writing skills in any profession they find themselves navigating.

---

9 Malcolm Gladwell, *Outliers: The Story of Success* (New York: Back Bay Books, 2011).

By providing interest-area modules at the click of a button, transitory curiosity can be engaged. Many times I came home from a party with a desire to research something because of a conversation I heard during the evening. In college I found myself sitting in lectures that were not in my field because of a conversation I had with a fraternity brother about a new subject. Curiosity, if pursued, often opens doors to a variety of offshoots that will, if allowed, lead a child into an interest area that can be of value both in their education and later careers.

WRITING AND READING

I'd like to offer a profound example of a voice that comes with the ability to express one's ideas in writing. A few years ago I was an instructor in the Bridge program at Antioch University Los Angeles. It is designed to help students who have fallen through the cracks. Some of our students were experiencing homelessness and some were returning from serving time in prison. All of them were in need of support.

As we approached the midpoint of the semester, I took a student I will call Terry aside and asked if I could help him, since he had not yet submitted any evidence of his work. I did this by recalling my own nervousness about the quality of my writing when I first enrolled at university. I had gone to a one-room schoolhouse for the first seven years of my education. We were moved to city schools for eighth grade, and all the small country schools were closed. I had managed to get to seventh grade with little attention paid to my education. I had a rich social life at school but little interest in sitting still and taking notes or practicing my penmanship. It was obvious in my writing that this was the case.

Even now I hate to sit still. Audiobooks were invented for people like me. I became successful in order to hire a secretary who could take dictation. By my early 20s I had found many ways to avoid being found out. I related to Terry in ways no one could have imagined, since I was a PhD candidate at that time. I asked Terry if I could type while he dictated his thoughts. At first he asked me not to type, because he wasn't sure of what he wanted to say. I assured him that it didn't cost us anything for me to type as he spoke. I promised that he could edit once we had the raw ideas down. He agreed, and we continued. We then walked to the printer to pick up his written document. Terry began to read and in the same moment, he began to cry. I realized in that moment that Terry, a 40-year-old man, had never seen his thoughts on paper. I can picture Terry, his emotional reaction, and his joy to this day. And it informs my commitment to helping students become effective at telling their story, expressing their opinions, and offering their thoughts in writing. There are worlds of possibility that open when you can express yourself in print.

I am blessed to have two children and two grandchildren who love to read. I often give books to friends' children as holiday gifts. One of my favorite bumper stickers is "So many books, so little time." For children, reading print will help inform spelling, sentence structure, and vocabulary. At my stage, I'm reading to enjoy the story; having a fabulous reader who reads the story to you makes a difference.

A few years ago I owned an acting school for children and teens. I began telling stories in the acting classes about what would make someone more attractive to a director than another actor. I would talk about the importance of reading the classics, so that you have a broad understanding of period literature. I assured them that a director would likely lean toward the actor who had read about a variety of time periods over an actor who was not a strong reader. I had several parents tell me that they were seeing a sudden interest in reading. This is meeting students where they are. I knew these kids wanted to act. I wanted them to read.

If a student isn't interested in reading on their own, find out what they are interested in and offer them items to read that engage that interest. Through reading about their interests, they are likely to stumble on careers and areas of study that will not only enhance their interest but also lead to meaningful work or graduate studies, depending on the child.

All of our students will need to learn how to type 50 words per minute. This alone is an important life skill and can easily be offered in the form of games. This is a module that is worked on daily until the required typing skill is achieved. The ability to engage the student in their education would be less of a struggle if they were getting back to a game rather than back to homework.

Typing is additionally a neurogenic exercise. It is also an easy win for the students. Even those most challenged by typing can, with time and practice, become proficient. These kinds of wins are beneficial in preparing for greater challenges.

HOW MUCH TIME SHOULD
WE SPEND ON EACH SUBJECT?

Students in our system will need less than three hours of screen time per day to complete their modules. These three hours are for engagement with individual modular lessons using the adaptive practice engine. Based on early research, these three hours will be equivalent to two to three days of classroom instruction with homework in a typical school. The three hours can be scheduled when the student is most productive, instead of when we choose to teach that subject.

You don't need a PhD to tell you that there is a lot of wasted time in the current classroom. As a personal anecdote I will share a story about my son in the early 1990s, when he was a junior in high school. His good friend was in a near-fatal car crash, and my son was spending every spare hour in the hospital with the friend, helping him stay up with his schoolwork and keeping his spirits up during multiple skin grafts for burns. My son asked me if he could attend a learn-at-your-own-pace school that was on his campus, so he could continue to be there for his friend. This school he wanted to transfer to was designed for problem students but did fit his needs at the time. I didn't want him to miss a crucial year of school. I didn't want him to be seen as a problem because he was enrolled in that school. I also didn't want to dampen the commitment he had to helping his friend.

This was in Los Angeles, where the high school culture rarely honored kindness, and I was proud of the approach my son was taking. In the end I agreed—with some requirements: He had to work on academics from 9 a.m. to noon with one snack break. He agreed, and to my astonishment he finished 11th and 12th grades in the four months remaining of that junior year. My only requirement had been those three academic hours, but in that time he saved a year for himself and managed to get his friend, who was a year ahead of him, through 12th grade. Students' ability to move through their studies at their own pace could resolve some of our classroom behavior issues that arise when students are bored.

This isn't just about letting a kid do the right thing by his friend; it is about letting kids find their interests and talents by jumping into new situations. Helping the student understand the difference between avoiding work and adjusting work to address new needs and challenges is what is required.

CREATING UNIQUE, STUDENT-CENTERED SCHEDULES

Much of our current system is developed around what is best for the administration, teachers, and students in age batches. Everything changes when you need to deliver information to a group. Nolan's program offers a chance to have a schedule that is student focused and adjustable and takes into account that a student will be drawn to a different system depending on their age, interest, and activities.

> Not all students have the same clock, even when they are the same age or playing the same sports. Some are early functioning and some later. To require all kids to work on algebra early in the morning will cause certain late-functioning students to struggle. That same student, if they are allowed to learn algebra in the afternoon, will have improved outcomes.

This is another important point. We know kids learn differently at different times of the day. Individuals do have different body clocks. Early risers have an advantage in school as we currently manage it. Research tells us that the majority of teens are at peak learning potential between 11 a.m. and 7 p.m., and yet we start most schools at 7:30 or 8 and end at 3, giving us only four of those eight hours to work with. Worse still, as Nolan mentioned regarding algebra, we teach core subjects to kids at times when they are least likely to learn and/or retain the information.

Some students need visuals, others need to hear or feel the content, and others will read and retain. This, too, we have known for decades, and yet schools have changed little as a result of this knowledge. Nolan's idea could address this need by the sheer amount of engagement by numerous senses and modalities at the time most advantageous to the student.

Again, the more senses you engage in the learning process, the better a student is at recall. As I've mentioned, Tony Buzan authored several books on the brain and has developed a system of note taking he refers to as "mind mapping," in which he engages color and free-form drawing with key words added to help with memory. According to Buzan's research, even word-for-word notes from a lecture will offer lower rates of recall than writing that includes pictures. Buzan encourages this practice in academics and in corporate meetings as an effective method of anchoring information.

We have tested some of our theories in games with extreme active-learning software. It is called adaptive practice. Our early software, which has been tested on 60,000 students, appears to teach at a rate that exceeds ten times faster than other methods and with better retention. The secret is that the software adapts to the student's speed and abilities and requires more than one action or mouse click per second. The activity is the key. When the thalamus is engaged through an act of will, the brain learns better and remembers longer. The information reviews are also spaced to make sure that the short-term memories are converted to long term.

continued

Today the typical learning mode is to have a week of lectures and reading with homework and then a test on Friday. Our software goes directly to the test, with immediate feedback. A wrong answer is as instructive as a correct one. The activity is the key. Since the software keeps track of which parts of the problem the student has difficulty with, it can return to the challenging area as often as necessary. The lesson does not stop until all material is learned.

We like to say that everyone gets an A with our software. The only difference is that some take longer than others. Even the differences between the slowest learners and fastest is relatively small; in an average population of students it was less than one standard deviation. It is also possible to match gifted students with other gifted students, or gifted students with struggling students to build empathy and to perfect the communications skills of the advanced students.

Kids who are accustomed to winning are often even more driven to excel when the competition is ramped up. I remember when my daughter, who had excellent work habits, came back after her first month at Berkeley and exclaimed, "This is really hard; everyone studies like I do. I have to really work just to survive."

There are some obvious benefits to an individualized learning method. Initially, the shame of being the last to grasp something in class is removed since the program doesn't shame or ridicule the student in the way the other students can or a teacher might on a bad day.

The school as a whole should be designed to maximize this goal of creating an environment that encourages all kids, keeping in mind that they will all be drawn to different elements of the offerings.

The individual modules will be the first indicator of special skills and attributes. The work done in a module will aggregate and create a blueprint of the students' strengths and areas in need of assistance. The makerspace, or play lab, and enrichment resources will allow a student to gravitate to something that is engaging.

It turns out kids like things they are good at. The challenge is to put in their path enough interesting and challenging experiences that both reward what has been gained and confirm their ability to learn. In this way, they are good at learning when they are not yet good at a task. In subtle ways, within games, we will test attitudes, preferences, and passions. The software can communicate many things that the student may not yet know about themselves. As the data on each student increases and connects the interests in various disciplines, a signature for that student will emerge. As a clearer picture forms, additional resources can be placed in the student's path. The educational world has never been so easily customized.

There is an opportunity to conduct longitudinal research that will offer insight and perhaps some answers to the questions around effectiveness of immediate intervention and the motivation informed by collecting trophies and rewards as the student moves through each modular level.

The fact that this educational platform prioritizes the interests and talents of each student makes it appealing to parents, teachers, and students. Helping the child identify their talents and expand on their interests to maximize those talents is a refreshing look at the future of education with individualized learning options. This has the potential to engage students in a way we have not often seen. This will inform the student's confidence about their potential as a result of being heard and appreciated for their talents.

Not only are students learning about themselves through the process of the modules and games, but also the teacher and parents are learning the talents of their child or student and can establish an educational plan that meets and helps the child maximize their potential. The amount of stress and friction removed from the family's life is significant and positively impacts the students' sense of their value.

There are a series of tricks that are used over and over in the video game world to keep children engaged and moving to the next level. These tricks can be employed to direct play and to allow a comparison with others but in a selected way to boost confidence and motivate the student at whatever level they are functioning in as long as they are moving forward.

School the way we have been doing it is failing our kids. Using what we have learned or could learn from the video game world makes sense if we are student centered. Yes, it will require that teachers drill down on their understanding of each student and how they learn, but with the burden of lectures and batch teaching being lifted, the teacher has time to spend with students in groups working on a project, and they have time for students individually when they are struggling or celebrating. So many students feel and have been told that they failed, yet the truth is that this is rarely the student's failure; it is the failure of the system.

PRINCIPLE #9.
FORM STUDENT START-UP
COMPANIES FOR AN EXPERIENCE OF
ENTREPRENEURSHIP AND COLLABORATION

The most important skill that any school can impart is the understanding of business and entrepreneurship. If a student understands entrepreneurship, they will never be unemployed. There is always something that can be done to make money. The companies are designed to give critical knowledge about company formation and the mindset that it takes to start a business. Let students try and fail a few times. There may be high stakes for them as students but low stakes in the world of financial repercussions. Entrepreneurship requires resilience and a commitment to learning from each downturn or failure. The same is true of their studies and the life ahead.

Student businesses will be set up to mimic a corporation with the students as shareholders. Each company will have a room as a headquarters. The president of the company can have his or her cubicle in headquarters.

Imagine that along one wall in the school are a series of offices for company headquarters. Each company has up to 15 members, including a student president, vice president of marketing, operations, finance, production, and sales. There are also some recruits who can either be paid hourly or can share in the profits. The companies are designed to operate as a business and make money. Each company will be responsible for financial reporting and company policies and guidelines. Some, such as waste management and cafeteria, will be standard services and operate as a service to the students and would be run by students, with students doing the purchasing, cooking, and serving, and operating all food operations, including renting the facility to other companies that could use it for their products like a Super Jam Company. Depending on the neighborhood, the kitchen might have an outdoor area with a service window to sell food or coffee to the employees of the businesses surrounding the campus.

Other companies will expand out of interests and explorations the students conduct and direct. One could be organized around selling on eBay. Products that are student designed and made could be among the offerings. There will be web-development companies and video game companies. Building products for the iPhone app store or Android is another possibility.

Each enterprise will require students to learn how to publish and distribute their product on a platform like Amazon. Some of our students will publish short stories, poetry, and music lyrics. Students are encouraged when they discover that a short story they wrote can be sold in bookstores. The amount raised isn't as important as the process the student engages in as they attempt to market their product. A sound studio will allow for audiobooks and podcasts to be produced and distributed for students interested in writing or narrating.

All students need to know how to market online. Knowing how online retail works is an important skill that may open up natural marketing talent. Because of the STEAM Lab Makerspace machines, a cool design for a laser cutter or CNC Router can be built and sold. The students can also operate the school store, selling T-shirts or other items to other students and the community at large. Some of the companies can be engaged in putting clever video productions on YouTube. Learning how advertising pays for a good YouTube video is a valuable life skill. Specific modules that are part of the enhanced curriculum will teach many of these skills.

These student companies will give firsthand experience of developing an idea from start-up, and in doing so will demystify the business-start-up process. Our students will graduate with the knowledge that there is a good deal of work, planning, and adjustment involved in starting a business.

My hope is that there will be several breakout businesses with kids experiencing some remarkable success. For example, earning an extra thousand dollars is a huge win for some students, and it will open their eyes to the potential of a good idea well marketed.

For every 300 students, we expect 20 companies to survive past graduation. It may be significantly more. In any case, the

continued

feeling of creating your own job will last for a lifetime. The ability to create your own work will be significant as an alternative to searching for a job in a down business cycle.

Every student will learn what it is like to make a payroll and to price a product to make a profit. Each will be able to earn money if their product can compete in an adult world. Kids, when given the tools, are amazingly creative and driven when they see that they can be making money by making things. Many kids think about a job in terms of a minimum wage. The idea of making your own job could be liberating.

The fact that most employees of Silicon Valley know someone personally who has started a company or joined a start-up and done well is an important part of Silicon Valley culture. That knowledge also gives a person the confidence to try their own thing. Remember that before someone starts something, they have to believe that they have a chance for success. Nothing works better than seeing a classmate succeed when it comes to planting the entrepreneurial seed in the rest of the group.

Every year the school will have a budget to supply small amounts of seed capital to the school companies. The budget can be expanded if the students are able to sell shares. This is a great way to engage families and friends who can purchase those shares. And the school website will have a store for additional sales. The school can also make microloans to fund projects and assist in funding for inventory once there are orders. Over time we expect to get businesses in the area to share expertise, resources, quantity buying, and unique machinery and perhaps provide venture capital to potentially interesting businesses.

Everyone involved in the school company has to learn a little accounting. Whether math is a strength or a struggle for a student, when math has relevance it prompts a stronger desire to understand and an increased ability to recall. Knowing how to balance a checkbook is a skill that every high school student needs for a successful life. This is how we start that habit. Seeing and paying bills can be daunting at first. Doing it under the guidance and tutelage of students and teachers you are working with on a school company can offer a depth of experience in running an organization that will scale with each student's career.

Today, being unemployed at some time in one's life is likely. We want our students to be aware that there is an alternative to looking for a job offered by someone else. You can create your own. If we can plant that idea in our students, the issue of long-term unemployment is altered for generations. If even a small percentage of the unemployed started a tiny enterprise, a recession would be a thing we read about in history books.

Creating a student-run business can be rewarding, and even if there is a failure, the experience offers a valuable learning opportunity and is less painful than investing everything you have in your first venture as an adult.

Nolan's idea is not as out of left field as some may think. There are numerous organizations like Junior Achievement that encourage students to plan a business and begin the process. This has rarely been part of school time. It has been considered part of extracurricular activities.

Nolan suggests that entrepreneurship is as important as the disciplines currently taught in middle and high school. Nolan, along with the Lemelson Foundation, suggests that we need not even wait until middle school, that elementary school students may well have ideas worthy of a business or invention.

A few years ago I was at the Paradigm Challenge annual event when they were giving out the prizes for student inventions. The age groups for submissions were 5–7, 8–12, and 13–18. One young woman in the 8–12 category won for her invention of a device to measure the lung capacity of a child being tested for asthma. Her premise was that the child would likely be nervous and not give a full reading of their lung potential when asked to blow in a medical device. Her invention was a dart gun that was connected to an app on the doctor's phone. The child was blowing at a target, playing a game. The results were considerably better with her device than the typical medical instrument. In her acceptance speech she said, "People are always saying that children are our future. We have ideas now; we don't want to wait for the future."

That was a wake-up call for me and was the rallying cry at the Lemelson Foundation's annual conference, which I attended later in that same year. I have no concern about making room for this kind of entrepreneurial exploration for students. There is no need to pressure a student into creating a business, but neither is there a need to discourage a student who would like to start a business or invent a product.

My next idea may be met with considerable pushback. What about rewarding students for a job well done? I realize there is a debate about the value of intrinsic versus extrinsic rewards. Clearly, intrinsic rewards centered on the feeling of happiness one gets from a job well done have a positive impact. But let's also consider something that may at first sound outrageous: What if we were to pay kids for accomplishing a module, for maintaining good grades, or for community engagement? What if we were to pay kids for their work?

Yes, the idea of paying kids for their work is controversial. But when you consider it in relation to their lives as adults, the question is less clouded. How many adults would show up for work with enthusiasm knowing there would be no pay at the end of the week or month and that they were not going to be paid for the job in any way? Keeping the intrinsic reward system healthy and adding extrinsic rewards could offer an interesting boost in engagement.

According to a 2019 article in *The Conversation*, written by Richard Holden, a group in Australia experimented with this idea.[10] They had 6,875 kids in the study. Students were paid for good behavior, for attendance (on a sliding scale), and the accomplishment of academic tasks. The year-long experiment showed an average of 17 percent increase in students scoring at or above grade level for the classes that were paid in the studied group.

The other noticeable outcome was that these students spent more time on the subjects and homework they were being paid to complete. In the group that was not paid for reading, those students' reading scores fell by the same 17 percent. Reward systems and their impact on student engagement and retention is an area that begs for more research.

---

10 "Richard Holden," *The Conversation*, accessed December 19, 2021, https://theconversation.com/profiles/richard-holden-118107.

Once we have an effective toolbox of projects and challenges that have been proven to work with our students, and we can repeat the test with the same results in other schools, then we can craft a strategy and a road map for any school interested in progressive educational methods.

$EDS AND BRIBES AS A TOOL

There have been many tests, both positive and negative, in outcome that measure the impact of incentives. The science behind reward systems is often muddy. What is clear from the various papers and tests is that incentives are complex, and one size does not fit all. This is the same premise that makes us move toward individualized learning systems.

Our first test is with the $Eds program. Much like tokens or tickets in Chuck E. Cheese, $Eds will be the basis for our reward system. Every module finished will deposit a hundred $Eds into the student's account. The student can then use the $Eds for digital purchases of time and freedoms, such as renting a video game or other entertainment options, which all will have an $Ed price.

Placement and upgrades of the student's workstation also require $Eds, and if a group of students wish to create a cubicle, there will be a cubicle charge. There will be enough desirable purchase possibilities that gaining more $Eds will be a motivating factor in helping the students take agency over their education.

Since modules are recursive, the remedial kids will have modules commensurate with their efforts. This will allow the struggling students to gain as many $Eds as advanced students, provided they have the same dedication to advancing. This system will attempt to use hidden rewards as often as possible to incentivize advancement to the next level.

So many organizations emphasize trophies and contests. It is our belief that contests can be more destructive than helpful, because we think that highlighting differences in outcomes may be destructive to the long-term self-image of the child who lags behind. Kids who are bright and super achievers are already motivated, while the slower and less passionate are further disfranchised by attention to their disability.

One of our goals with students is to prepare them for life as an adult. Having as close to a real-world experience in education can help address that goal. Incentives are a key part of corporate life, entrepreneurial ventures, and even family management. Having incentives as leverage is not uncommon with parents negotiating with teenage children.

We are faced with the same opportunities on behalf of the students in our care. If a child is passionate about something in middle school, and they become curious about the topic, shouldn't we be making it possible for that student to explore everything around that topic or interest? The interest could lead to a business or product or an author they want to follow. Helping support the interest and direct the student toward accumulating knowledge will impact future work and options for future work. It is also an opportunity to help the student learn to sort through what is important and what warrants the time and attention needed to build their knowledge. A business or developing the product now or in the future will require that of the child. If a child's age indicates that they should be in seventh grade but they are interested in concepts taught in twelfth grade, how do we accommodate that child and encourage their potential? If a child is interested in starting that business as a child, what do we need to prepare them with and for?

$Eds earned on coursework can be used to support any entrepreneurial venture. It is an incentive. It is money earned by the student for work the student has accomplished. Incentives are sometimes intrinsic but not always, and rewards are a driver and motivator for many.

Our students will also have ample opportunities to display their work, not the least of which will be a yearly program in which all student projects will be represented. These will either be in its completed form or as a work in progress with a summary on why the project has been undertaken, what stage it is in, and, in some cases, why it was abandoned or redirected.

A foundational requirement at the MIT Media Lab are demo days where projects are demonstrated. It's a big motivator and a way for the lab to remain relevant.

Similarly, we will celebrate effort and self-evaluation. Current realities will dictate a digital gallery, but the future may offer a mixture of in-person and digital venues to experience individual and group projects. This is also an opportunity for the students to pitch their idea and look for seed money to launch a product or service.

Wherever possible we will attempt to level the playing field so that any student, no matter their circumstance, finds they can thrive. The main reason that there is no homework on our platform is that many kids have no real place at home that is well lit or quiet enough for homework. Some live in a small apartment with poor lighting and perhaps a blaring television with siblings fighting over who picks the show. There are even homework-hostile households.

These conditions are not only toxic but also further disenfranchise a student who wants to better their circumstances and career potential through education.

Even in homes where homework is possible and concentration is encouraged, there is a benefit to helping students get their tasks accomplished during the day so they can be kids and enjoy their interests in the evening and weekends.

We have a generation or two of people who think that working 17-hour days and taking work home on the weekends is what you need to do to be successful. Offering students a chance to unwind and decompress on the weekends may positively impact this issue for future generations.

TRANSCRIPTS AND MODULES

In the schools of the future, I'd like to see the students, not the school, own their transcripts. The information included in the transcripts will include the module attainment

continued

information, which will give granular details about the students' proficiency and academic accomplishments. Along with a certificate of graduation from high school and/or college would be a complete listing of modules finished. This will be a better indication of the education and skills acquired by the student than typical report cards.

The student should control the security of this record and grant access to potential employers as they see fit. Each module provider would grant a digital certificate that authenticates completion to prevent fraud. In this world of block chain and smart contracts that prove the speed of mastery, the question is, "How far can the module education go?"

For an employer, it would be helpful to be able to quickly scan a group of job applicants for particular skills. Additionally, there is usually a need within an organization for shorthand evaluations. We believe that our plan can address that. Perhaps in the future a person could communicate their education as an ordered set of numbers. For example, suppose we were to separate modules into five categories: science, math, humanities, arts, and business. The person might indicate their modules in the various fields as follows:

A person who says that they are 57328 is telling us that they completed more than 5,000 modules in science, 7,000 in math, 3,000 in humanities, 2,000 in the arts, and 8,000 in business. Immediately you would know that this would be a person who could work well in a scientific business.

The modules will identify progress over a lifetime, as different interests emerge and the adult continues to engage in the modules to update their knowledge about their field of endeavor.

Can the modules plus one-on-one mentoring give a student the experience of critical thinking that a really good professor with a small class of students discussing issues in depth can supply? This is certainly one of the key questions to be addressed in the research.

As Nolan mentioned, educators and potential employers or investors could tell a great deal about a student by the number of modules completed in each academic discipline. Nolan also advocates a commitment to update and continually add to the module system, hoping that students will reengage at different stages of their life post-formal education. After a year of everyone's becoming familiar with digital platforms like Zoom and Facebook, we can further explore personal relationships in the digital world and perhaps better compare the use of a digital platform with having a strong professor or teacher in the child's life.

> What is the real difference in education between a Stanford graduate and one from Humboldt State? Clearly, many of the benefits of Stanford, Harvard, or Columbia are the friendships and relationships between students.

The pandemic has created new ideas about how we educate students and will have a lasting impact on the future of this current group of students. It can be a positive impact or a deficit if we miss the opportunity to rethink the way we are educating the next generation. Much of what Nolan suggests is radical and yet rings true as a method of engaging students in their academic life and beyond.

As parents and educators, our task is to ignite the interest in a young mind. Their interest, not ours. The best way we have seen to do this is to expose them to as much as possible early in their life. Let the child explore every topic they land on with interest. If they don't have any interest in the topic when they start, move on to the next. Have them write about what is interesting or why it isn't of interest.

CHAPTER 8

Sharing User Experiences

The stories in this section are not accounts of things that have happened. As we've noted before, user experiences are journeys of imagination, what we think real life would be like if the concepts and proposals we've outlined came to pass. The users in this chapter are composite characters based on information gained from a wide variety of interviews, human-interest pieces, and academic research. They help us envision what the school of the future would be like.

ERIC: A HIGH SCHOOL HISTORY TEACHER'S TALE

I have been a history teacher for more than 20 years, and I love my job. Over the years I've come to learn that I have a special knack for engaging my students. My students become passionate about history while in my classes.

continued

I was introduced to the ExoDexa system a few months ago and have been intrigued ever since. I'm confident that I can bring my subjects alive in modules, just as I do in the classroom, and I love the idea of being able to touch thousands of kids at once and turn them on to a love of history. I am also very intrigued by the ability of the ExoDexa testing data to demonstrate unequivocally which techniques work best.

I have noticed that there are many people submitting math and science modules to the ExoDexa store, while very few have been submitted for my area of specialty, and yet history modules are just as needed as math and science ones. Since the purchase quantities and the student ratings of modules are published, it is easy to calculate how much the module creators are earning. It seems to me that almost anyone who is submitting a module is earning about $500 per month per module, and when a subject is taught over a year, the earnings come to about $1,000.

I realize that if the sales are this high after a few months, without having any public schools signed up yet, the sales are going to get better and better. I know that I have skills and knowledge in enough areas to be able to create about 50 strong modules. I am pretty sure that I could complete a module a week while teaching, and two a week during the summer.

By the time I launch all 50, I would bet that the average number of students in the program will exceed 50,000. I was thrilled to realize that if my 50 modules were used by all 50,000 students, I could make $2.5 million per year by teaching school! Of course I understand that my modules would need to be the best, or at least fit a particular learning style in order to stay in the top rank where all the money is made, but I'm confident that since I will be getting in early, I will have a jump on everyone else and will quickly master the best techniques to keep my kids learning quickly.

In my reviews of the most successful modules, I've been amazed to notice that although the modules are designed to take the average student 15 to 20 minutes to complete, I would actually need material from two to three days' worth of normal lesson plans to match what is covered in each module. This has made me realize how much time is wasted in the classroom; no matter how hard you try, it just can't be very efficient when there are 30 kids involved! I figure that the constant testing also engages the kids who would usually have been daydreaming most of the period.

I have also been amazed to observe what has taken place with the algebra modules over the months. The competition for Algebra I is fierce, and it has been paying off. The average completion times have dropped by three minutes per module in just the last two months! Imagine if every kid used the most efficient module, it would shave many hours off every kid's time in algebra class. That time would have been wasted in a less-efficient system, and it certainly is being wasted in most classrooms! I've even heard some educators say that the modules already are twice as effective as normal classroom teaching.

Here is another possibility: I used to be a Boy Scout leader, and I think that some modules on leadership and enthusiasm

continued

might be fun to develop. I have always appreciated the Boy Scout merit badge system, and I believe that specialized skills should be put into modules as a way for kids to earn extra credit. I think I will get in touch with ExoDexa to find out the plan for this type of nontraditional academic learning. After all, with kids finishing high school perhaps a few years early, they will have plenty of time for new skills!

And one final thought—last year I taught night classes at a local junior college, and now I realize that under the ExoDexa plan, there is no reason why the kids who complete the normal high school–level modules could not continue on with college-level course modules. This would be a wonderful opportunity for many advanced students!

What usually concerns teachers about individualized learning is the workload on the educator. In this scenario, the extra work is done by software, leaving the teachers open to create modules. There are few educators who would argue against individualized lessons from the point of view of effectiveness. We know what one-on-one learning does for a student with tutoring, therapy, and music lessons. Applying that to academics through software offers great potential. Nolan's expectation is that we will see an increase in interest in self-directed learning and a heightened self-confidence in students.

Computers don't have an attitude. They don't have bad days or lose patience when dealing with difficult students. There is no embarrassment when the student doesn't understand or messes up on a paper, nothing comparable to stumbling on a word when reading aloud to the class. The learner can celebrate their progress with less worry about how others are viewing each milestone.

Recently in a conversation with a group of women, all of whom had grown children and grandchildren, I heard one mother comfort a younger mother concerned about the pace of her child's learning with a reflection of her own experience with a child who was a slow learner. The older mother described what it was like to raise a child who walked later than others, talked later, and struggled in elementary school. She described a neighbor who frequently compared this woman's slower child with her own son, who walked at 11 months and was talking early too. This boy was an athlete in high school and always came out ahead in those comparisons. What was the end of the story? The slow learner is now a medical doctor, while the neighbor visits her son in prison.

We know some things about a child who is an early learner but not everything. We know that if a child hasn't learned to read by the third grade, we are more likely to see that child enter the penal system than others in their age range who love reading. Grades are still necessary, because of the way we measure growth and ability, but they don't tell us everything we need to know.

BEN: A CURIOUS STUDENT'S STORY

I noticed on my way to school that there was an outcropping of rock that looked very strange, and it got me wondering what had caused all the layers and waves in the rock. I talked to my teacher, and she suggested an early module on geology. I started on it and was hooked right away.

It turns out that the rock in my neighborhood was once part of a big lake floor millions of years ago. The layers are sediment

continued

that was laid down, as a river brought in clay and sand, which formed the layers. As the land was pushed and reformed, it was lifted up so that those layers are now almost vertical. I am sure now that there is a fault nearby and that there may be an earthquake on it someday. There is a module on earthquakes and volcanoes that I am going to do next. I never thought that rocks could be so interesting. I even get $Eds for doing this. So awesome!

From the student's point of view, there is time to explore interests large and small. There is time for building on ideas in the day-to-day schedule. If something catches a student's attention, the plan is to encourage their exploration. This is one of the ways we can keep curiosity alive. If the child is scolded and asked to focus on the task at hand, we lose the opportunity to engage that student where they are. And where are most students? Playing a video game or hanging with friends or watching videos about stuff they are interested in exploring. If a computer-based system can allow room for this kind of self-directed study, we will have gotten over a significant hurdle.

EVETA FROM RUSSIA: A CLASSMATE FOR KIDS IN CALIFORNIA

I live in St. Petersburg, but every night I talk to my friends in California. They say they have adopted me into their school.

My English is getting better, and both Chloe and Ryan are getting better with their Russian accents than I would have expected. They are really cool friends, and we plan to get together either this summer or next. I want to go to college in the US, but I would not be able to afford it. They say that they will help me find a scholarship because of all the help I am giving them; that would be my dream come true.

Trying to make more money, I am actually writing a module on Russian slang and swear words. This was not my idea, but Chloe and Ryan say that everyone should know the slang and how to cuss in the language they are learning. I agree with the slang but am not so sure about the swearing. They talked to the headmaster, who agreed that the slang was a good idea but that the cursing should be part of a separate module they call a trinket.

A trinket is a short module that has a small set of learning items that are usually just for satisfying curiosity. The slang project has been fun, and I actually find that there are more Russian slang words than I thought!

In addition to the cultural advantages of long-distance teaching, learning a foreign language opens new pathways in the brain, in part since so much time is dedicated to training the mind to recognize new sounds.

Nolan has mentioned that having a German living in Germany as a language coach could enhance the learner's experience because of the inclusion of cultural experiences in the language. With that lens, the ability to have students working closely with students in the native country, and learning languages using modern interpretation software, offers a deeper connection and understanding of the others' culture.

JEROME: A FORMER GANGBANGER

When I look back at the guy I was three months ago, I can't believe who I've become. Three months ago I was a gang member and frequent drug user and seller. No doubt I was a real badass, and no one messed with me at school; even the teachers were afraid of me. I was sent out of class to the dean of students—"the warden" as I called him—every week.

Since I always did funny things and didn't care about getting busted, I was pretty popular, even though I dropped out of sports. I never did homework and always made fun of kids lugging their heavy books home. I even tossed a little kid's backpack into a dumpster and sat on the lid till the kid started to cry. I guess I went too far.

I was 16 and in a class with 13- and 14-year-old students. I couldn't read. My first years in school are kind of a blur. Back then, my mom had a boyfriend who I hated. He hated me too. I never wanted to be home, and that was fine with him, I guess with her too. Doing anything to get away, I started to hang on the street with my friends all the time. We found an old shack and fixed it up and called it our clubhouse. We would spend hours talking, getting beer if we could, and just hanging. I was selling pot to make some extra money and smoked some of my stash. School was something I had to do, but I never paid attention, and no one ever seemed to care that I didn't learn. Reading seemed silly, and every time I tried, the words would not come.

Eventually, I decided to drop out, since school was such a waste of time. I really looked forward to telling my old "friend," the dean, that he could take his school and shove it. But it turns out he didn't look so surprised, and instead he actually ended up surprising me.

He asked if I knew what I was doing with my life, and I told him my life was shit and that school would not help me make it less shitty. This is when he surprised me. He said that there was a new school down the road and that he would try to get me in. I figured he meant it was one of those "special" schools and told him there was no way I would ever go there; my friends would never let me live it down. He said it wasn't like that and that I should try it. He told me that it was a really different school with lots of video games and that I could always drop out after a couple of weeks if I wanted.

The video game part sounded cool—my mom never bought them for me, and only a few friends had them—and I also figured there might be some new hot girls to meet there. I can always make girls laugh and like me when I want.

I knew the minute I got to the school that this place was different. There were no classrooms. Instead there was a big room full

continued

of machines. It actually looked more like an office than a school. There were computer screens everywhere and drawings all over the walls—actually *on* the walls, not just on paper on the walls.

Now I'm pretty good with a spray can and have decorated my share of buildings and walls, but it's never been legal before. But here, when I was shown to my cubicle, they told me that I could decorate it any way I wanted. The next thing that surprised me was how much was going on. People were walking around and talking; everyone seemed busy and happy. This all seemed very suspect; this couldn't really be a school.

I put on the earphones and started my computer and was shocked when it greeted me by name. No one cared about my name before, but now even a computer knew who I was? Then I remembered the wristband they gave me when I first got here and realized that there was some kind of chip in it that the computer could detect. I have never used a computer except to play games at the houses of the few friends who have them. I'm good at games.

Words that I couldn't read flashed on the screen. They stayed there a minute and then a voice in the headset said that if I didn't know the answer I should touch the screen on the red blinking square. I did that, and then another screen popped up and the meanest dude I have ever seen came on the screen. He had a shaved head and was all tatted up with what looked like prison tats—you know the kind that you do yourself with a needle and ink—and said to me, "What's the problem?"

Now this is the sort of dude that you never ignore, so I just said the truth and admitted I couldn't read. He said, "I thought so. I think I can teach you how to read in about two months." By now I really figured I must be in some sort of candid camera skit, so I just kept going with it.

I told him that I was 16, had been in school for 10 years, and it hadn't worked out so well. But then he smiled at me and told me that when he was 16 he couldn't read either, and because of that he did a bunch of stupid things and ended up in prison. And then he told me that he was *still* in prison and was talking to me from there! Damn, this was so weird. But I had to admit that I was curious.

This was a guy who I thought could understand me. I asked how they let him talk to teens on the outside. Wasn't that a security violation or something? He told me that he had seen the light and was now trying to help as many of us young shit-heads so that we wouldn't do the things he did. Yes, this new teacher of mine actually called me a "young shithead."

I asked him his name, and he said, "Call me Moses." It was the first time an adult male had seemed interested in me, except for me to do some shitty job or to run drugs. The reality is that Moses was right; he told me how to load some reading lessons, and sure enough I was starting to read basic stuff in a week and was quickly getting better and better. Anytime I got stuck, Moses was just a click away. I really liked him; he was the tough-est guy I had ever seen, but he seemed to really want to help me. It was totally strange, but, honestly, the school is pretty cool.

When I got more comfortable with reading, I found that I

continued

actually liked it. Lots of my lessons had me reading comic books and stuff that was nothing like what the other school wanted us to read. It was like watching a movie in my head. The best part is that Moses and I started to talk about life and what my life could be. Recently he asked me what I liked to do and I said that I could draw and that some of the best graffiti in the canal downtown was mine. He told me about a new lesson to load; he said to do it today and to tell him tomorrow what I thought of it.

I loaded the module and found that it was a hopped-up drawing program. The teacher in the room brought me a device that had a pen, and whatever I drew on the tablet would appear on the screen. I learned all the tools, and it made drawing faster. Then it dumped me into a program called Photoshop. That one was even more superpowered, and I was totally hooked.

I wanted to play with Photoshop all the time, but the computer would make me finish other lessons first sometimes. That sucked, but it wasn't really so bad, because the reading was coming more easily and the other modules were sort of fun too. And doing all those modules gave me more access to Photoshop, so I was cool with it. My drawing was definitely getting better.

One day I got a message that turned out to be a request for me to do a certain type of graphic. I did it in a few minutes and sent it back. Then I got another and then another. My computer dinged, and there on the screen was a geeky white kid who said that he was very impressed with my drawings and asked me if I wanted a part-time job a few nights a week and all day Saturday. He said he was from DreamWorks and that he would pay me

$20 per hour. I thought he was joking. He wasn't. I had never even had a minimum-wage job, and now I would be making more than my mom. He said that I have a great career ahead of me; I hope he's right. This school and Moses have changed my life.

I had the opportunity to work with the producers of *Redemption: the Stan Tookie Williams Story*. This young man's story reminds me of Tookie, but it offers an optimistic view of what can happen when there is positive intervention. Jerome's story illustrates the trajectory of a student's life when it's tweaked by caring adults. Educators become educators to have an impact on students like Jerome.

As we've noted, students benefit the most from one-on-one attention to their issues and their education. That is pretty impactful for the educator as well. It is essential that we learn to meet the child where they are without judgment or expectations. There is no room in this system for judgment by other students or the coach/mentor/educator.

When a child is behind, only the instructor and the child know. And if a child is behind, it is up to us to help them find their way to where they need to be in order to move to the next level in their studies. If they have not learned to read, we have not found the topic that will pique their interest and drive them to read. A child's interest in a subject is the reason they read. They read so they can learn more about what they are interested in.

We spend a lot of time on the techniques of reading and less time looking for what will motivate the child to want to read. In the very young years, you do this by reading to the child and also reading for your own interest in front of the child. If a child has reached school age without this influence, they have a tougher time finding their way to a love of reading for the sake of learning or even just to read and escape into a story. That is often the benefit that comes from the early exposure to reading. Without that, we need to find the student's interest to drive the desire to read.

In this learning environment, where the software alerts the educator to a struggling child, the problem can be addressed before the child knows there is a problem. The system does it in a way that preserves self-esteem.

> When a teacher is notified by the system that there is a child in peril, the child gets a note from the teacher asking how the day is going and offering the child an opportunity to express the frustration from their perspective.

Ultimately, that is what we want: for education to be in the child's control. We ask questions to find out what the child sees as the problem. Do they think they are not smart enough to understand? Do they see it as a flaw in the question? Or somewhere in between.

If we didn't have to spend time teaching a lesson to 30 students with varying levels of ability, we could spend that time drilling down when needed with each child. The educator's job is to understand where the child is in their educational journey and then to support them. This is also an opportunity to build a portfolio of information for the teachers/coaches/mentors to easily access that will assist them in understanding how best to support a given child. This is where record keeping is essential.

> What we know about a child enhances our ability to respond as effectively as possible when the child presents with a need. If a child is keenly interested in sports or music or a particular

animal, we would know that in an instant. The more meaningful information about emotional challenges, celebrations, and complementary studies or interests in this child's learning, the better our chance of reaching them. This information will all be available to the adult taking part in a one-on-one with the student.

Some of this may sound very idealistic or even fanciful to many readers. I assure you that there is a path from where we are in education to where we want to be for this next generation.

How do we support students' differences and celebrate their advancement at whatever rate it happens? There are so many variables that will inspire curiosity and suffocate the same. If we can help students protect their curiosity or embrace their ability to be curious, I think we may have the beginning ingredients needed to raise a generation of thoughtful problem solvers.

BART: LEARNING CHINESE WHILE EXERCISING—AND USING VOCABULARY TO SECURE A LUNCH DATE

I'm usually at school around 7:30 a.m.—never thought I'd choose to come to school so early!—but this morning traffic was good, so I got here even earlier than normal. I hit up my cube, pulled out my headset and bio transceiver from my locker, put them on, and, boom, I was online.

continued

A children's story in Chinese started to play as I entered the locker room and picked up a pair of shorts and socks. I changed and then moved to the warm-up area just as the first set of comprehension questions came over the headset. Sounds pretty high-tech right? See, my headband is a Wi-Fi–linked system that connects me to the school's central computer system. Last night, I'd chosen the Chinese lesson to do this morning. With the headset and through voice commands I can do some modules while exercising. I often like to do Chinese while exercising. It's a pretty easy thing to practice while doing something else, since much of the early lessons are about repetition and listening to pronunciation.

This morning I first did the comprehension test by answering into the microphone attached to the headband; I can do that while stretching. This device is awesome; there is even a bio transceiver connected to my headband, and via Bluetooth it gives the central computer a constant monitoring of my heart rate, skin temp, breathing, and blood pressure. Total *Minority Report* stuff.

Anyway, I started to jog and listened to the Chinese story. Not to brag too much, but I'm honestly a bit amazed at myself. I mean, I can understand lots of this tough language after less than four weeks of drills! Sure, my speaking and writing are pretty terrible, but my vocab is growing by at least 20 words a day; it's really adding up.

Another awesome thing—my Chinese mentor lives in a small city in the Xian province in central China, and mentoring me and other students is his second job. He also works the night shift as a math instructor in a Chinese college. Though he's supposed to just be my Chinese tutor, I asked him for some help with precalculus recently, because I thought he might be good at that too, and it turns out that he had a very different way of explaining it that was actually really helpful.

So back to the morning… I was jogging on the school track and listening to my Chinese story, and I noticed a hot girl on the track in front of me. That was strange, because I know everyone here, but I didn't recognize her. Picking up my pace, I passed her, turned around to look… and almost tripped. It was Jennifer Woods from my old school, but, to be honest, she definitely hadn't been that hot back then. She had been a little overweight, with lots of acne, but now she was totally toned and glowing. Damn, she's hot!

Just then the second pop quiz of my Chinese lesson started, and I realized that I had totally tuned out—I don't have a clue what had been happening in the last part of the story. I backed up the lesson to the point at which Jennifer had totally distracted me, but that's okay because suddenly I had so much energy I ended up running a few extra laps, because I was totally feeling it and because I wanted to finish the Chinese story.

Once finished, I hit the showers, feeling pretty pleased with myself. I earned max points for the morning, plus I also got extra points because of multitasking my exercise and Chinese. Sweet!

After the shower I brewed up some green tea—we all drink it here; it's supposed to do something cool to your brain—and

continued

checked my email and calendar. I've got a class at 10 a.m., a company meeting at 3, and basketball practice at 4. Not such a bad day! I know, because I organized it that way; we can do that when we earn enough $Eds.

Before jumping in, I read a few articles about some new movies and video games, and then settled in for some fun with calculus. I know that sounds crazy, but this calc module is awesome. It's like entering another world. It's hard to describe, but the module is an environment that deals with adding up smaller and smaller slices of things and then representing the process with numbers and symbols.

For some reason, these tools work for me, and I can solve lots of problems this way, which then lets me access even more interesting and complex worlds. I actually had precalc at my old school and failed it. But, really, only the name was the same; this is a totally different calculus.

After about 20 minutes of calculus world, I stopped when the computer suggested a break; funny, how did the computer know I was getting antsy? I stretched, talked a bit with my friend in the cube next to me, and then hit up the module again. For the most part the teachers here trust us to make our own breaks; it's cool. And the modules are actually fun enough that we all end up being pretty trustworthy! A shock, I know.

Case in point: I got back into the module after that little break and managed to knock down two barriers, which opened a gate giving me access to some of the sweetest worlds yet. It is so cool. I maxed the spot quizzes and felt really good about the huge number of $Eds I'm racking up in the upper right side of my screen.

I haven't decided what I'm going to spend the credits on, but I'm considering using them for music and zoning. I also like the idea of renting a larger cube to combine with a couple of my friends. You can do that here, if you earn enough $Eds to get it. Of course buying food and drinks is always a good possibility. Lots of students use $Eds for "stamps" on IMs to other students, but I never do because we can actually send messages for free if we work the weekly vocab words into them. I kind of like the challenge and like saving up my creds for really important things.

That got me thinking . . . maybe I'd get to work on this week's vocab words and send Jennifer Woods a message seeing if she's up for lunch together. Here is my creation:

"Hey, Jennifer! I saw you on the track this morning and remembered you from Mr. Johnson's class at Paul Revere Jr. last year. Let's catch up! Want to meet for lunch today? It could be a harbinger (vocabulary) of good things to come and be a way to make my sphygmomanometer (vocabulary) reading go off the charts."

I have to admit that I was pretty impressed at my use of vocab. I mean, who incorporates a sphygmomanometer into an IM?? I might have set a record. Maybe it's a little lame, but I hope she'll find it kind of funny. Either way the extra credit for the two vocab words was worth it. Ha ha, it's funny how my

continued

thinking has changed; before I never would have risked doing anything that might not seem cool, but at this school I don't really worry about it. Everyone here is sort of cool in their own weird way.

My computer dinged a few minutes later. Jennifer wrote back, "Sure. I'd love to catch up. While masticating (vocabulary word) our food, we could have a dialogue (vocabulary word) about lots of stuff. Without being presumptive (vocabulary word), can I ask when and where?"

I thought it was really cool that she used three words in one message. You can get a bonus if you use all weekly words in messages that week; I bet she is going for that bonus. So it seems that I need to step up my game. Now I need to construct a message using the rest of the vocab words. They are tough too: penumbra, exorcise, perambulate, castigate, and photon.

But then inspiration flashed.

"As you perambulate to the table closest to Madagascar, please block the photons from the window, so that I can bask in your penumbra. Halloween is coming up, so let's talk about us pairing up to exorcise and castigate any evil lurking that night."

Clicking send, I got three dings and a gong—five words in a single email and the full vocabulary module done for the week. Plus got lunch with Jennifer coming up. It's like a super win.

It is no surprise that Bart is motivated and influenced by the interest of a young woman. Every successful person I know credits their love interest or interest in love for their youthful career choices. That seems to be true regardless of sexual preference; our love interests are a draw.

Sustaining that interest once the girl rejects him or the allure wears off is the challenge. Start with the fact that the student is motivated to be where they are. Adding items to the treasure chest in a game—and metaphorically as the student builds relationships with mentors, educators, and other students—the draw to be a part of projects, inventions, and events may help keep the student engaged.

PETER JENSEN: SCIENCE TEACHER

I am shocked at how much having the right equipment makes a difference to my students. I've been teaching about plant types—genus, phylum, etc.—for years, but letting the kids actually plant seeds, ferns, and mosses and grow mushrooms brought the lessons to life in a way I've never before witnessed. Even growing tomatoes and basil for the school kitchen for a profit has turned kids on.

Applying their learning to the real world makes a huge difference to these kids. The other day I was amazed to see that when a group of students saw firsthand the mass of mycelium that is necessary to grow a mushroom, it brought home the understanding that the mushroom is just the spore bearing fruit. I was thrilled to see them excited to learn that by collecting the spores and putting them in a cool, damp, and dark place with humus, the spores will grow much more quickly.

continued

The chemistry hood and other equipment makes learning about pH and chemical bonds fun for the kids and gives context to what they are learning. The advanced kids who want to learn about bioengineering are fascinated by what can be done with simple used lab gear that was purchased for just a few hundred dollars. The spectrum-analysis machine teaches more about how the spectral emission of a molecule gives us understanding of what atoms make up a sample than I ever could in my lectures.

Lenses and electronics mean more when kids use them to invent things; even simple low-power lasers can make the world come alive. I actually find that I, too, am learning through these lessons. I find myself researching things just like I did in college. The Play Room, as they call it, is playing for me as much as for the kids, and I believe the students sense my excitement. I think we all engage with each other with enthusiasm more than I have seen in the past.

I find that I am using almost every spare minute outside of school to build new modules so that the kids are even better prepared to use the equipment and tools. I get the same questions over and over again, and I know that the students will remember the info better if it comes from a module and hands-on training.

I am sure that I can even turn on some kids who think they hate chemistry and biology; with a good module that is fun and exciting, it's a completely different ball game. Each student I motivate gives me an amazing sense of accomplishment, but it's awe inspiring to think that with this new module system I could potentially reach thousands of kids that I will never even meet. I want to give it a try; I know I can do it.

Teachers are motivated by the idea of impact. They want their work to mean something. To a certain degree, a teacher made this choice over high-paying jobs in finance or industry in order to impact the next generation. What ExoDexa proposes for teachers will be a motivator for many. Teachers who are considered outstanding in their discipline will have an opportunity to reach students well beyond the walls of their school. And, as a bonus, they will be paid handsomely for that work.

JOHN: AN EMERGING DIRECTOR

I had always thought that I wanted to be a great film producer or director. In my new school, I finally got my chance to create a short film that I wrote, directed, and shot. My friends acted in it, and I edited it with Final Cut; I even got great encouragement from my teacher, who is a former director himself. But when it was all finished, and I watched it, I was horrified. The timing was wrong, the music was wrong, and the whole thing just didn't work. I was really embarrassed that I could think I would ever be good at this. I didn't want anyone to see it, but my teacher insisted. He watched it and said, "That is

continued

the best first try I have ever seen." He said that he had seen Steven Spielberg's first attempt, and this was clearly better. I was shocked.

My teacher said that the most important thing that any student can do is to have a beginner's mind. I had no idea what he meant, but he pointed to a sign on the wall of his cubicle, which I had never noticed before. It said, "Be an Elegant Beginner." He said that everyone is horrible when they start something new and that the horribleness is part of the learning process.

He then went on to say that if I kept at it, by the end of the year I would be making some really great things. He warned me that my next one would probably not be too good either, but that it would be better after my having gone through the process the first time. He said that he would go through each scene and make suggestions. He also pointed me to some useful websites and lent me a copy of *The Lean Forward Moment* by Norman Hollyn that was dog-eared and obviously well used. He said that it was the bible for any filmmaker. I thanked him and went home to read. Now, after being so discouraged, I am suddenly more determined than ever; I will master this art and someday win an Oscar.

JIM: A ROBOT CREATOR AND DESIGNER

I have always wanted to have a robot. And it's totally cool that now I can actually build one myself. My robot is small, but every day I am making him smarter. I didn't realize how much we humans rely on our senses. Compared to us, robots are pretty stupid and almost blind. I am adding every sensor I can, because a robot needs to see, feel, and hear to be able to do anything.

Since starting to work on the robot, one of my teachers has been telling me about an event called a maker fair, where people like me can show off personal inventions. I'm going to enter my robot into the competition; I think I can win at least some of the events.

I didn't know any programming languages before coming to this school, but even though I'm new at it, I'm picking up robotics pretty quickly. I guess it comes naturally to me. The more complex stuff is still beyond me, but I'm working on it! In fact, the scripting language I'm using now is already starting to feel limited.

Python is the next language I should learn. It seems strange to have to learn new programming languages all the time, and it's a lot of work, but I guess that's what allows the really good guys to always build such new cool stuff. Python lets you do a whole bunch of things, particularly with vision, which is something that my robot will really need help with.

continued

I don't have a camera on my bot yet, but as soon as I do I'll be needing a bunch of the open-source applications Python has so that my robot will be able to interpret what he is seeing. I know I am not good enough to do that on my own, and I know my teacher can't do it either, but I'm pretty sure that he can hook me up with an expert who will help me.

My girlfriend is helping me with the robot's personality. At first I thought that the idea of giving him a personality was dumb, but of course I didn't say that to her, and now I have to admit that when I hear all the smart things my robot says, it's actually a huge part of what makes him so cool. And I may have to quit calling my robot "him," because my girlfriend gave it a female voice. I am not sure I like that, but it's fun to work together and create our own little person. Ugh, that makes it sound like we are way too old; I'll think of it as a little puppy instead.

For the last decade, I have been part of a movement with educators encouraging a change from the lecture style or, as Nolan put it, "from the sage on the stage to the guide on the side." We want teachers to prompt students rather than instruct them. Kids learn more if they have to research and adjust to ideas that didn't pan out. Our role is initially to help them ask better questions. Later it is to help them test their product or theory. This all works best when the student knows what they are excited about or interested in and we just need to coax in that direction. Some students don't know what their passion is.

John, the emerging film director, knew what he wanted to do when he arrived at school. Part of this exploration requires that the student be an active participant. They should have a say in the choices and direction of their learning. Also, it helps if we can get them active in a project. Learning by doing isn't just a catchy phrase, it is a philosophy of education. Some students will be ready to take on their own project, and others will want a little time before they are in that position.

That student can first assist the student who is already working on a project. Sometimes it could be a related interest that draws the student to another's project, and other times it may be the team that student wants to work with that brings them to a project. There is very little pressure in this position and plenty of exposure to learning opportunities. It also offers room for the student to dive into their own interests and ideas and develop their own personal project. There is some privacy in the exploration stage for the student to contemplate various interests and future projects, pick something, and also change their mind.

Students should all be encouraged to change when they are inspired to change an idea, a philosophy, or a standard belief, if they are confronted with science or logic that defies their platform. Students should be taught that changing your position based on facts is a positive experience. One of my favorite comments from the Dalai Lama is: "If Buddhism and Science differ, Buddhism must adjust."

BETH: BRITTANY'S MOM

I can't even begin to tell you how concerned I was about putting Britt in this crazy school. It didn't look like a school or act like a school, and when I visited, it seemed like there was nothing but chaos. Well, maybe chaos is going a bit far, but I couldn't imagine how anything efficient was going on. All I saw were people walking around, talking, and joking.

continued

And the walls were covered with everything! In fact there were so many things to look at, I stumbled and almost fell over a small robot that was rolling down an aisle. A red-faced teen apologized and said that he was going to activate a higher alert signal so that this didn't happen again. He said that he was working on perfecting "Don" and that the robot was too quiet and he was worried that people would be bumping into it all the time, just like I did. I guess I proved his worry.

I entered a back area and asked a girl near the door the direction to the headmaster. She said that they had the best headmaster under the sun and smiled. Well, that was nice and all, but I needed to know where to find him. I asked again where he was, and she smiled again and said, "Under the sun." Just before I got mad at this impudent girl, I noticed that I was under a large model of Neptune and then I got the joke. The headmaster's office was in fact under a model of the sun, though the "office" was simply a cubicle like all the others, albeit a bit larger.

When the headmaster greeted me, he said that he had gone over Britt's transcript and application. He touched a screen in front of him, and Britt's materials appeared on-screen. I started to explain that Britt's grades were not an indication of how bright she was and that she had gotten in with a bad bunch of kids, etc., etc.

He said that he didn't care what she had or hadn't done last year and that he only cared about who she was at her core. That seemed strange. He then showed me the tests that Britt had taken as part of the entrance process and told me that he thought Britt was quite sad and that the most important thing we could do is to improve her attitude. I almost fell out of my chair.

He said that everything improves if attitudes and optimism are uplifted. He then asked about me and my husband, and I told him that I had been working as an assistant in a law firm and that I was divorced and had been for the last seven years. He then gave me a homework assignment and a password to the parents' portion of the website. He said that in order to keep Britt in the school I had to check that parents' site five times a week and follow the instructions it gave to the letter.

I knew I was asking for it, but I thought I had to be honest. I blurted out, "Britt smokes pot." He smiled and responded that, of course, he knew that. It is all over her answers, he said. He said that they could help that, too. "But how will you do that?" I asked. I felt that I had tried everything.

The headmaster said, "Kids can function, but not very well, if they are smoking pot every day. Pot is about trying to get away from life. Life has hard edges, and pot simply softens things. When people are excited about life, they like that hardness and clarity. When kids start to smoke, they don't see the things they lose. They are worse at video games, they are worse in school, and their life becomes mushy. Kids stop smoking pot when there are more fun things to do, and, yes, their peer group is important. Fitting in is crucial at these ages.

continued

"We enroll each pot smoker into a special test program. We ask them to participate in a test-of-skills program that we are doing for a nonprofit foundation. As part of that program, we simply ask them to take some quick tests each day and to indicate when and how much they smoked in the previous 24 hours. We stress that their answers are encrypted and that no one at the school or anywhere else can access the identity of the test subject. After two weeks we ask them to go cold turkey without pot for two weeks and to continue to take the tests each day. The foundation requires that a urine test be taken at the end of the two weeks to assure accuracy.

"We then demonstrate with graphs the difference in their functioning between their two data samples and illustrate some interesting likely effects on their lives, incomes, and creativity between their pot self and their straight self.

"The system is not 100 percent, but in almost every case the pot use at least decreases. And in most of the kids it stops entirely when the student becomes engaged and passionate in one or more of the activities in the school."

I was sold. Now a year later it has actually played out as the headmaster predicted. Britt is passionate about many things again; she loves art and dance and her friends. She thinks about her possible futures and is even so intrigued by several of them that she cannot decide what she wants. I tell her that she doesn't have to decide now and that she should continue to explore. I am thrilled that she is dreaming; I never want her to stop.

Most successful adults can tell you the first time they knew someone really believed in them. That person was often a teacher. This story of Brittany reminds me of a student I worked with who often was high when she came to class. I knew she was bright, her class participation was sharper on some days than others, but it was always obvious that she clearly had what it would take to complete her degree. It took more than a year to gain her confidence and be able to address the topic of her pot use without sounding like a judge. I knew by the way she received the conversation that she was able to take in my comments, and time would tell what she would do with it.

A few years later I saw her and had my answer. She had confidence I had not seen in her as a student. She told me then that our relationship had a profound impact on her current life. She was grateful, and I was grateful for that moment.

It can be the smallest thing you say to a child at the right moment that can move them in one direction or another. In most cases that means that the educator has offered positive input and evidence of belief in the child dozens of times before one lands in a way that inspires the student. Believing in a child is the greatest gift you can give them as an educator. If you can help them see in themselves what you see in them, that begins a pattern of positive self-talk that can guide the person through a lifetime of issues.

It only works if the educator genuinely sees the best in the student, and we as a collective society should only hire educators who have that potential.

BETTY: A DAY IN THE LIFE OF A FASHIONISTA

Hi, my name is Betty, and I am the fashionista to end all fashionistas. I love clothes and simply can't get enough of shoes;

continued

my BFF, Ashley, thinks I was made to be cool. Ashley and I spend every penny we have on things to wear.

Since coming to this school, I am in the STEAM Lab Makerspace as much as I can be, working on my own clothing designs. I never thought that I would become a computer geek, but there is this really cool program that makes it easy to design clothes based on my own fabulous fashion sense. I'll admit that some of my first designs came from a magazine, but there's nothing wrong with that. For example, earlier this year I totally fell in love with an amazing dress that my favorite actress wore to the Oscars. Of course, I had to have one just like it. The problem was that it was like $30,000 from the designer. Yeah, right.

Lucky for me, I am super awesome and don't need to buy a dress. As part of one of our projects, Ms. Milly gave me a budget for fabric and took me and some other students to the garment district. We went to this warehouse that had like a gazillion bolts of fabric. I picked out some that I totally loved, and it cost practically nothing. It wasn't exactly the same fabric as the Oscar dress, but I actually liked it better. My dress will be cooler for sure. I was amazed that I could buy enough fabric to make an Oscar-worthy dress for less than the cost of a T-shirt at the Gap. I was totally so hooked on this project (and I couldn't believe I was getting school credit for it) that I could hardly get through my other lessons fast enough to get back to the STEAM Lab Makerspace.

When the dress was finished, I put it on and asked my friends what they thought. Everyone loved it, except that jerk Martha who doesn't like anything I do. I then went up to Bart, the hunk, and could totally tell that he liked the dress. Of course, he just stood there like a Greek God not saying anything; he never says much. But then he said, "Wow." He actually said Wow! I'm sure that was the coolest thing he had ever said to anyone.

Then I had the best idea ever. What would a Greek goddess of love wear if she were to capture the heart of a Greek god? I did a quick Greek goddess internet search on my computer and actually found some patterns for a gown. Bart doesn't stand a chance.

Just then, Margaret came into my cubicle and asked if I would make her a dress like the one I had on. Then came my second-best idea ever. I certainly didn't want her to have the same dress as me, so I said that she could buy mine and that I would give her a good price. I told her that I had another design in mind anyway. I knew that making the goddess gown would take another trip to the fabric store, and I also needed money for shoes, a clutch, and jewelry to go with it. I gave her a price that was about a third of what a dress like this would cost in a store (a knockoff version, not the actual designer version), and she said yes almost immediately! I must have priced it too low, but even at this price, I made way more than enough to pay for all the accessories and the new fabric I would need.

I talked to Ms. Milly about my plans for the goddess dress, and she suggested that I actually make the shoes, clutch, and jewelry. I looked at her like she had lost her mind, but she said

continued

that Greek goddesses wore simple sandals and that she could show me how to cut the required pieces on the laser cutter and to finish them with the other tools. We could use the same process for the clutch and jewelry. I am so game and can *not* wait to get started tomorrow. Fashion designer world, watch out— Betty's comin' on the scene!

I wish more kids had this kind of confidence. This is what we are aiming for when I emphasize the importance of engaging kids where they are and building on that interest. Betty learned so many new skills in order to accomplish her goal, which is very different from learning a list of skills that are on the syllabus. Once a child has a goal or an interest, it is going to be hard to get them to think about anything else. Let's use that passion to teach them how to learn.

SALLY: PRESIDENT OF SALLY'S JAMS AND JELLIES

I like to cook, and my mom and I made jelly this summer. It was the best jelly I have ever tasted, and we thought it would make some cool holiday presents. When I came to the school, I found out that we could start companies and make stuff and sell it and earn credit.

I knew instantly that it was time for the world to taste Sally's Jam. We have a commercial kitchen that has all the needed permits, and my teacher said that he would help us meet the health regulations and that it was a good idea. I took a module on company formation and downloaded the documents and formed the company. It was so simple I was totally shocked. Though I didn't understand all the things in a document called the bylaws, my teacher said that I would over time.

The strangest thing was how all at once I had one million shares in my company even though it just started. I then asked my best friends to join my company and offered to give them shares. My teacher said that I couldn't just give shares, that there had to be consideration. He explained that no one, even me, got free shares. We all had to buy them. This got stranger and stranger, since I didn't know what to charge. He said that usually a penny per share was a good number and that usually at this school the president bought $25 worth and the other officers bought between $5 and $10. We became investors. We also had a three-member board of directors and a real company.

My teacher wanted to invest and said that the school would also, because others had tasted the jam and thought it was a good idea. He also said that we had made so much progress that the shares were worth more. Now both he and the school would invest at $.05 cents per share. I was totally shocked. In two days my shares were worth $125. The school had a special deal with the bank, and we got a company checking account and a set of books. It turns out that for every expense we have to code the check into a category. It was very confusing as to what was capital equipment or research or inventory, but my teacher said that at first it is always confusing.

continued

We needed bottles and a label. I asked one of the students who was a great artist to design the label. He tasted the jam and asked if he could work for stock. The teacher said it was okay, but we needed to have a little contract. He showed me how the deal was done. I loved the labels, but in looking at commercial jam bottles, I realized that I had to put ingredients on the label and some snappy names. Jill was the most marketing savvy of our group; she was vice president of marketing. She had a whole bunch of ideas that turned my little company into a multiple product company with seven flavors that had names but had not yet been invented. She found a website that had very cool bottles, but, wow, they were expensive.

As we solved problem after problem, things started to make sense. My teacher said that we should keep notes about what types of jam were available commercially and what companies charged. He said that most products in a grocery store had about 25–30 percent markup and that things in boutiques were at 50–100 percent. He said that we should focus on the boutique market and to find a niche.

I thought that making really good jam was enough, but he pointed out that everyone said that their jam was the best and that the bottle and marketing material had to say something more, something unique. This was a whole new way of thinking. In fact, the original reason for doing our jam was that I thought that just being good was enough. My company was taking on a life of its own.

We faced our first crisis. It turned out the minimum order from the bottle company was 144 bottles. The bottle we had chosen cost $.60 each. That used up all the money of the company and left nothing for the fruit and ingredients. I also found out that we had to rent the kitchen. That seemed a little cheap on the school's part, but those were the rules. My teacher said that it was important to make the company behave like the real world. Whatever.

The school said that it would give us a loan for inventory but only if I had an order. I had two bottles of the jam that my mom and I had made, though without the labels or the right bottles. But Jim, who runs the company that operates the school store, said he wanted any product made by the school and that school products were easy to sell to the parents.

Jill and I made a presentation to Jim and let him taste our sample and told him about our seven flavors. He said that he thought that he could get $6 per bottle and that he needed a 100 percent markup. I was really mad. We had to buy the bottles and fruit to do the work and he would make more in margin than we would. It was not fair.

He also said that we had to take returns if someone complained. He was being a total jerk. I had kind of liked him before this, but now he was just a jerk. I told him it was not fair, and he simply said that he had been doing this for a while and it was normal. He said it was just business and that it would be worse out in the world. He said he would pay in 30 days from shipment. We really didn't have a quick alternative, and

continued

we said okay. He handed us a purchase order, and we went back and showed it to our teacher. Jim had given us an order for 24 bottles of each flavor. I realized it was an order for $504. Even at the lower price we charged, it was going to make the company more than $300 in profit. The school lent us the inventory money, and we set to work.

First came research. We now had to develop the new recipes and flavors. We had cool names, but now we had to make them. Our idea was to make spiced jams. It took us more than two weeks and about 30 small batches to come up with our flavors, and by then we thought we really had something. We had everyone taste them and got a lot of enthusiasm. One kid's mom ran a little specialty boutique, and he said that she would give us an order. It was the same size as Jim's. We now had over a thousand dollars in orders.

We did one batch each day and put the labels on by hand, and in about two weeks we were ready to deliver.

We got time off from school and made some sales calls. We now had finished samples, and in one week we had sold more than $5,000 in jam. The work was getting really heavy so we decided to hire our first employee. It was a big step.

We were really in business.

Everything that Sally learned to accomplish is easily transferable to any company or career she decides to pursue. It also has the added benefit of giving her an income while she explores any other area of interest. This isn't going to be true for every student, but it will be for enough of them that it is a welcome consideration for the curriculum. Student companies offer an opportunity to build empathy working with staff (fellow students) and to develop a sense for logic as a result of running a business.

Some students will have no interest in taking on such a monumental task; others will be inspired to chase their own passion. Either way, if a student becomes more self-aware, the process is effective.

MARY: A CONFUSED TEEN

I am worried about being different. While all the other girls here in high school are obsessed with boys, I really don't care about them. I think I might be a lesbian. Of course I've never told anyone; it's so hard to even admit that to myself. My dad will have a fit if he even thinks I might be, as he says, "deviant." He takes me to church every Sunday, but I would never talk to anyone there. It's definitely not okay to be gay there. But I know that I have to talk to someone or I will go crazy. I have some big questions, and I don't have anyone I trust enough to ask. I want a normal life, I want to fit in. I'm scared.

I just noticed on the school website menu that my school has doctors and psychologists who can be reached anonymously via our private computers. Maybe if I reach out to one I can get some answers that will help me, or I'll meet someone I can talk to about this. I am going to do it tomorrow afternoon; no one will know. I'm feeling pretty scared, but thank God I've got this option—not every kid does. I don't know what I'd do otherwise.

This is another area in which a student's ability to explore an idea or a problem with some sense of confidentiality is important. A student who has the room to ask questions, seek counsel, or just find an educated ear to listen will be more likely to seek that guidance than a student who believes that if they speak up, the whole world will know their business.

I don't know many people between 12 and 16 who want to draw attention to themselves. That is a stage at which you are doing the opposite, and trying to keep attention off yourself can be a full-time gig at this age. Social and emotional learning and health are important enough for a school to have policies around and, in the best situations, to have staff ready to jump in when needed.

DAVID: AN EXCEPTIONAL
STUDENT OF HIGH-LEVEL PHYSICS

I am very excited to go to school every day. In my old school I was bored to tears, and it just kept getting worse. My physics teacher was a nice enough guy, but he knew about as much about physics as I did when I was 10. He tried hard, but he didn't have the advantages that I had. See, my dad works for NASA's Jet Propulsion Laboratory and has a PhD in chemistry and physics. He's brilliant. My mom is a researcher in genetics but actually only has a master's degree, a circumstance for which she jokingly (I hope) blames me. Evidently she was getting ready for her orals when she got pregnant with me. When my friends come over for dinner, they say that my family talks in a different language. I guess most families don't talk about physics or genetics at the dinner table.

I realize now that we have talked about really interesting things for as long as I can remember. I know that I understood quarks by the time I was ten (if anyone ever really understands quarks). And I also now know that I have had a home life that always encouraged learning, which certainly helped me develop my potential. That meant that school was always boring, because it just couldn't compare. Now it is anything but boring.

I have decided that I want to do research into nanotechnology, which means that I have to know a huge amount of math, physics, and chemistry. I chose nanotechnology because I am great at all those subjects, although at the beginning I was still a little frustrated because I wanted to get past the silly simple stuff into things that were really hard and challenging. That all changed three weeks ago.

I completed all the math, chemistry, and physics modules in about six weeks, which my mentor said had never been done before. I thought that school was going to get boring again, but then a bearded and slightly mean-looking guy popped up on my screen. In a very thick Russian accent, he asked me what I wanted to know about physics. I was at a loss for words, but then I thought, what the hell, I'll ask him about something my dad was talking about the night before. It was related to dark matter and antimatter.

Mr. Russian Dude raised one eyebrow, and we got into it. Wow, did we ever! I felt that I was drinking from a fire hose. He was not just knowledgeable about the subject, he actually had some theories of his own that I had never heard. I know that my

continued

dad would love this guy. I think he was surprised that I knew as much as I did, but he never talked down to me. Being treated like a peer from someone this smart was a real ego boost.

That first session lasted about an hour, and afterward he said that we could get together three times a week, but that the sessions would probably have to be shorter because he was working with other students too. Then he also suggested that we set up a group conference with "physics kids from all over the world." He said that the time-zone differences could be a pain, but he thought that we all needed to know each other. He said that some of the sessions would be in Russian and some in German, but that most could be in English. I decided that I would learn Russian as soon as I could. I already had some pretty good German under my belt.

I started the Russian module that afternoon and found to my oh-so-pleasant surprise that I would be tutored by the hottest Russian girl I have ever seen. She lives in St. Petersburg, and the deal is that she wants help with her pronunciation and vocabulary in English, so we decided to talk in Russian for half the session and in English the other half. The first session was awesome, and I really looked forward to the next session.

The way this school is organized is terrific. In my old school I would have had to wait for a new quarter or semester to get started on new topics with new teachers, and there would be a bunch of crap I would have to do to get into the class I wanted and to fit it in with my other classes. Here when I want to learn something, I just click on it, and the rest just seems to happen. I am sure there is some wizard behind a curtain making this happen, but whatever is going on, I sure like it.

This kind of program is really ideal for a student like David. Students who pick up on subjects easily and are motivated to learn more are the easiest to teach in an independent learning environment. One rarely even needs to clear the path for these students; just don't get in the way. School as usual gets in the way. Encouraging a student to explore an interest or research a new idea they were exposed to . . . this is where education is the richest.

PASTOR JOHN O'DONNELL: A DESIRE TO ESTABLISH A SCHOOL

I run a small church in a town of 10,000 people, and my congregation has been pushing me to start a school for their children. We have a nice facility with classrooms and a gym that is unused most of the week. None of my congregation members are rich enough to put their kids into the only private school in town, which charges $25,000 per year. One of the elders brought in a brochure for the ExoDexa School System and said that he would lead the fundraising committee to pay the franchise fees to bring it to our town. He said that there are enough

continued

kids in the congregation alone to fill the school but thought it would express good citizenship to allow anyone to enroll. He felt that most of the people could afford $9,000 per student and that there would be enough left over to provide some of the needy families with a full or partial scholarship. It seems like he has it all worked out, and I think it may be a very moral thing for this church to do.

I could be the headmaster, further saving money, but I would need to have some good teachers to really do the teaching. I graduated from college and have a master's degree in divinity, but that was many years ago. I may have to do some brushing up. I know that there is a push to have vouchers in this state for parents who want to send their kids to private schools, and I can get behind that proposal; it would certainly make it easier for everyone. We have a state ecumenical convention next month, and I am convinced that if we all work together we have a really good chance of getting the referendum passed.

The published results of this new school system are amazing; in fact, they sound too good to be true. I will research it and pray on it and see what answer comes to me.

The year 2020 gave us a view of how much we need to work together on education. Parents became educators, and educators became "on-camera talent" as a result of distance learning. We want to bring students back together, but perhaps the bringing back needs to be restructured to have smaller groups of students gathered in interest pods and project pods instead of batched by age. The different age groups may need different types of help and supervision, but I do think that Nolan's proposal for the school of the future addresses much of this. A parish, a synagogue, or a community center are all potential classrooms for when we want to bring students together.

MARY RODRIGO: A HEADMASTER FOR A DIVERSE STUDENT BODY

I have been a school administrator for the last ten years, after having started my career as a high school history teacher. I thought that I had seen everything in a school that was possible to see. I have seen some of the best, as well as the worst, teachers. I have seen kids thrive and fail. I used to think that the problem was the kids and their parents. I was wrong. *We* make a difference.

This school has something for everyone. For the most part, even the kids that I would have wagered would drop out before the end of the year seem to find themselves.

Before coming here, I was the principal at a high school just down the road. We had 3,000 kids, a dropout rate of 40 percent, and only 35 percent had grade-level literacy. The rules and bureaucracy left me no freedom to apply my own judgment. I was incredibly limited in my ability to take action against some truly deficient teachers. I knew that the combination of certain bad teachers and certain at-risk kids would lead to a dropout

continued

as predictably as the sun coming up each day. How any thinking or caring government could allow this system to ruin life
after life without taking action is totally baffling. I care about
students, but I simply could not serve them the way I wanted in
the current public system.

This new school has 600 students and is the second school
I've seen using the ExoDexa platform. It is in a difficult section of Los Angeles, and we have a student body that is like
the United Nations, with students who are African American,
Latinx, Chinese, Korean, Pakistani, South Asian, and a few
native Caucasians. Over half do not speak English at home,
and many have parents who cannot read or write English.

My old school had roughly the same makeup. The students
are the same, the area is the same, but what a difference the
ExoDexa school is making! It is the middle of November, and
by this time in my old school I would have had at least 30 students drop out. In this school I have had one. I am sure I will
have more by the end of the year, but I cannot easily identify
which ones. Perhaps I actually won't have any others.

Many of the students in this school came from my old school;
I even know some of them from their repeated visits to the
office for discipline. I understand that the admin here wanted
to test this system against the one I previously ran, especially
since it's in the same neighborhood and so many of the external
elements are the same. I suspect that the admin folks wanted
to hire a principal from a local school, in order to further limit
the variables between the two schools. Truthfully, that might

be how I got this position. But, either way, I guess it ultimately doesn't matter; I am very happy here and I want to stay.

One of the reasons I had thought that there would be a high number of dropouts is that I knew that many of the students were extremely poor readers. At this school, students can't hide like they do in normal schools, and I expected those students with a poor educational foundation not to be able to cope with the system knowing their weakness.

However, so far the opposite is true. In fact, if I believe the testing metrics, this school started with the same rate of grade-level literacy as my old school but has now increased it to 45 percent; this happened in just two months. At this rate we should be in the high 70s by the end of this school year. I have never seen this much reading advancement in so little time. I guess the software is pushing that over any other subject, since it has detected that as the biggest weakness of most students. I love that the software can do that on its own and that it can address each student's needs individually.

But perhaps my biggest shock is the number of really talented and smart kids who are here, especially since, as I noted, many of them are the same kids as at the old school. I've known some of these kids for a few years, and somehow their talents were invisible before. I know that some of the kids didn't want to be geeky or perceived to be smart, but were they purposely doing poorly on the tests? The way the software is structured, it is hard to fake results, and no one knows the results but the student, the teachers, and the administration.

continued

The kids can even hide it from their parents if they wish. I am continuously shocked to realize that some kids actually feel the need to do that. This is something that most schools and teachers do not understand and can't work around.

All our teachers are making more money than before. The physics teacher here has developed a top-rated module that, for homeschooled kids alone, is earning him more than $80,000 a year. Speaking of teachers, I am going to have to replace one of them. I bring this up because it's important to note that in this system teachers are selected based on their ability to teach, and that ability is in large part determined by the students themselves. Since the grading is all done by the tests and the one-on-one relationship with the student is voluntarily determined by the student, they do not want to waste their time on a teacher who is ineffective.

I am amazed how quickly word spreads about the teachers who help versus the ones who are a waste of time. The good teachers find that they have a waiting list, while the poor ones soon find they are quite lonely. Even if a poor teacher tries to intervene while watching one of his students, the student can opt to continue with the software and not get help from the teacher. The number of turndowns is another very telling metric of how kids feel about a teacher.

Some teachers find that they feel powerless without the threat of grades. Others find it a refreshing loss of an annoying burden. So far I have noticed that the more a teacher complains about the loss of grading power, the less effective that person is as a teacher. Good teachers appear to be rewarded simply by helping a student understand something.

Perhaps the biggest difference in my job is my budget. I have money to spend on special projects, and the numbers are always in the black. I knew how much was being spent before and somehow there is more here, even though the base numbers per student are the same. ExoDexa has purposely used the same budget numbers so that the comparisons are fair. Still, somehow the amount of money available seems to be much greater. I guess my ability to direct it to where it is most needed and to remove a dysfunctional teacher helps enormously.

Our budget for the year is $4.2 million. The income includes summer school and some tutoring income. Our average cost for the school year is $7,000 per student. We have a great deal on the facility rent, and our average teacher salary is $55,000 a year, which is slightly lower than the average at Los Angeles Unified. The main reason for the lower salary is that the staff is younger than most mainstream teachers; the younger ones tend to be more open to the avant-garde teaching techniques. Also the pension benefits are different here; the retirement age is 65, just like for other workers, not 50–55, as in most school districts. Our teacher-student ratio is slightly higher because of the demands of individual coaching.

Despite the slightly lower base salary, most of the teachers are actually earning more than they would have in the public sector. That is because many do extra shifts in the tutoring section and some are writing modules. Since the students have

continued

no homework, and the teachers have no homework to correct each day, the teachers find they have much more free time to do these things on the side. Our teachers are much happier with their job, salary, and benefits than any teachers I have ever worked with.

At the old school, there were a huge number of interracial fights, but so far there have been none here. I think the daily exercise takes the edge off the kids' tempers and has also really helped to change the atmosphere. Most of the sullenness that was always present before is gone. The kids look healthier, and, maybe because they are more self-assured, the student body is less self-segregated than before. I think there is much less drug use, though we do not drug test unless the kids volunteer for "The Program."

I work closely with the special headmaster, who is in charge of all the nonstandard parts of the business. He has used the facility resources for after-school programs for tutoring and projects with kids who are not students of the school. He also fills the school on the weekends, holidays, and school breaks with kids who want some extra learning. With all these programs, he earned almost $2 million in additional revenue for the school. I choose not to run the summer school because I have always taken summers off to spend with my own children and to travel. I could have chosen to earn more money, but the time with my own children is important to me.

I feel like I have the greatest job in the world; I am having fun and am finally making a difference. That dream is why I

> decided to become an educator all those years ago, but I have
> never felt that I was able to do so until now.

So much of this rings true. I know that I'm repeating myself, but engagement is the key, and helping students find interests to explore will inform their engagement.

WENDY: A YOUNG ENTREPRENEUR

I hate to admit this, but I used to be a moody bitch. I guess it was because I was never very excited about anything, but now that has changed. When I first started at this school, I thought that the games that they had us do at the beginning of the day and at random times during the day were totally stupid, but I did them anyway and for some reason I started to feel better—happier and more calm. I didn't notice this at first; I was just doing the activities because it was more trouble to fight against doing them, but over the weeks I started to realize that I was actually looking forward to those silly games, and that visiting certain places in the games made me really happy.

I've never really traveled. My family doesn't have much money, so vacations were never our thing. I don't think my parents have seen much of the world either. But it turns out that

continued

some really awesome places aren't even that far away. I live in California, so getting to Yosemite wouldn't be too expensive. In fact, I talked to my dad about wanting to go, and he said that the weather probably wasn't very good now but in the spring the waterfalls are really spectacular. He told me that he had gone camping there as a kid with his family and loved it. Then he got a little sad, and I think he was feeling guilty for not thinking to take me before. I guess we all get stuck in a rut sometimes, not just me.

I had always figured that I wouldn't like camping, but now I actually think it could be fun—dirt, bugs, and all. Even my mom thought it was a good idea but said that one or two nights was probably her max, because she would need a shower after that. No worries, Mom, I think I'm with you on that one.

The Grand Canyon is also close, and I think we can do that pretty easily also. Not everything would be so easy, though. I really liked Rome and the south of Italy, but it's expensive to go there so I probably have to wait a bit on that trip. On the plus side, though, my teacher said that the school was looking into organizing a summer trip to Europe for the students, if they could make it cheap enough.

That sounded fabulous. He said that some of the school businesses had offered to put their profits into the travel fund, and that if they were successful it might be cheaper than expected. I know that the kitchen company has been making some decent coin catering for some professional businesses in the area and that the kids had a couple of jobs that earned them more than a thousand dollars! Also the day care center is full, and I know it's pretty profitable too.

My company is selling cool T-shirts on eBay and on the school website. We were just starting to get orders, but we make $7 in profit per shirt, so I know there is good potential there. I'll get to work on thinking up some new cool designs and hopefully that will help. I have always been good with images, but it wasn't high on my priority list. Now making money to go to Rome would be worth the extra effort for sure!

We are in the business of inspiring kids to want to know something. Here we have a kid with a goal to make enough money to go to Rome. Wendy is learning budgeting, geography, and anything else to research this interest. Wendy wants to go to Rome. How can we help make it relevant to her education? It is on us as educators to help our students ask effective questions, ideally by modeling that behavior.

DR. EVERETT MORGAN: RESEARCHER

I have just received a grant to study how intelligence differs among individuals and have an agreement with ExoDexa to use its data-collection system to collect real-world results. I will collect and create a series of tests that are designed to assign a numerical value to each of the nine categories of brain function. Understanding divergence of intelligence will help us

continued

build platforms that target the style of learning that best supports each student.

We will attempt to find out the variability and to correlate the data with actual results in a series of tests that are meant to track potential success in a variety of fields.

I have been doing learning and cognitive research for more than ten years and find that the type of information that has been so expensive and difficult to obtain is now available at a very low cost. My special tests are added in seamlessly and cost very little. It seems that one of the student-run companies in the ExoDexa school has been given the right to market the data as part of its company.

They are neat kids, but they are pricing their data much more cheaply than any other source would. They were adamant that any results I get are theirs to use to increase their system and methodology. I am going to publish, so that is an easy request to agree to. I will also give them access to my base research and the backup documentation, so that they will be able to reconstruct my findings. No one else will get that data.

I hope to have several of my graduate students use these schools to research other areas. These days the field of learning, and the mind-body link with learning and understanding, is exploding, and I want my university to be at the vanguard.

The science of learning and brain neurogenesis is just starting. Knowing more about how the brain grows and increases capability is within our grasp. We need hard science with precise data that are reproducible. A lab where test subjects are students is the only way to get good-quality data. And it will help them and all the students that come after them.

I have read the plans for all the things that will be studied, and I'm very excited to be a part of it. I am going to a conference on learning and the brain and believe that I can interest my colleagues in this pursuit. With enough resources pushed in this direction, we can truly make kids smarter and more successful over their whole lives. Increased creativity and higher IQ will help everyone.

WHAT WE OFFER WITH EXODEXA

So much of what ExoDexa offers is born of the meeting of the minds of parents, educators, and researchers trying to have a positive impact on the way we educate our kids. We have been conducting professional development workshops through the Two Bit Circus Foundation, LA Makerspace, and Trash for Teaching for the last eight years in multiple school districts. We're encouraging teachers to move from teaching to facilitating, to giving a prompt that will send the student in search of an answer, rather than giving them the facts to memorize for a later date. One of these paths promotes critical thinking, and one does not. We need this generation of children to be capable of critical and creative thinking to solve problems they will face. We need to make changes in education in order to encourage this way of teaching and thinking.

If the technology Nolan describes is possible, individualized education is a fast next step. It is a step that will be welcomed by educators, parents, and students. It offers educators the ability to work with individualized learning with the heavy lift on technology and online platforms. It offers instant feedback to the student. Parents have their own portal that offers a day-by-day understanding of what the school is engaging in and expecting from the students. Individualized information about their student would be handled first in a discussion with that student, engaging the parents only when deemed necessary. If a student is in trouble with their work or emotionally and needs help, there is support. Even if the help is remote, backup is built into the system.

Encouraging students to take agency over their education requires a plan and the ability to follow through on that plan. The closer the student is to creating their own plan, the better the chances of their sticking with it. That is in line with what research tells us happens when an individual is engaged in choosing goals and agreeing to them.

CHAPTER 9

Nolan's Blueprint for ExoDexa Schools

N ot everyone using the ExoDexa system will be able to remodel or redesign their entire campus. For those who can, Nolan's design and schedule for the ideal ExoDexa school program follows, including ideas for how inner-city schools can accommodate Monday-to-Friday school.

Let's begin with the structure of the school day. In our school it looks something like this and is implemented from 8:00 a.m. to 5:00 p.m.

- 8:00 a.m. till 8:30 a.m.—Aggressive physical exercise integrated with light audio lessons and review

- 8:30 a.m. till 9:00 a.m.—A balanced carbohydrates-and-protein breakfast

- 9:00 a.m. till 12:00 p.m.—STEAM Lab Makerspace, projects, corporations, discussion groups, or cubicle time

- 12:00 p.m. till 12:45 p.m.—Lunch

- 12:45 p.m. till 1:15 p.m.—Nap time

- 1:15 p.m. till 2:15 p.m.—Aggressive physical exercise with integrated light lessons

- 2:15 p.m. till 5:00 p.m.—STEAM Lab Makerspace, projects, corporations, discussion groups, or cubicle time.

REDESIGN THE SCHOOL BUILDING

The next step is to redesign the physical plant. Most current schools can be made to fit this new model. At most, a few extra hours of staff will be required, and some walls will need to be removed. The biggest change will be to have fewer traditional classrooms and more learning spaces that inspire educators and students.

Overlaying the above are the requirements that any good system needs to be self-healing and self-improving. We will establish effective feedback loops, with the student council taking part in decisions made about the campus. We know that whatever we figure out today, there will be a better way tomorrow. This system is established with that in mind. The speed to which the newest and best is deployed into the population is important. Research will identify if there is an impact on efficacy.

In the event something is effective, we will repeat it and scale the program. With real-time research we can also adjust when something is not working.

The best way to deploy an effective idea is to have empirical evidence that is shared widely in the academic community. In the school of the future, the best practices and modules are dispersed to students automatically and designed to match the students' interests. No bureaucracy. And again, we will hear from the students about their experience and on how we adjust for students coming up behind them. We will engage students in the conversation about what is missing and what they would recommend for the physical school of the future.

The second requirement is that the school cannot rely on massive inputs of additional money. Pie-in-the-sky systems that are not cost effective simply mean that the deployment is delayed or thwarted entirely. We think that current educational budgets are more than sufficient to create these superschools.

THE PHYSICAL SCHOOL OF THE FUTURE

The balance of this book will be about how this school of the future works, how it is funded, and how it looks and feels to the student, faculty, and families. It is not sufficient to have grand goals; we need a plan. Execution must be possible or it all falls apart. Things will change, but if the bones of the system are sound, our outcomes will prove its value.

What does the campus look like? Our plan is to make the physical space a learning experience for the students. It's not just a space in which to learn but also an opportunity to help the students build their relationship with their school and take agency over their education.

The Sign Out Front

The first thing we all see as we approach the campus is the sign. In front of every school will be a sign that has the name of the local school and below it "An ExoDexa-Powered High School" or Junior High. It will have four geometric shapes that are three feet in all dimensions. They are a sphere, a cube, a cone, and a tetrahedron. Below each is a place for a name.

Each week four students are tasked to paint the shapes. The only rule is that the end result cannot be a repeat of color or layout from anything that has been done before. The four students can coordinate their designs or simply do their own thing and bring them together for placement. Their name is on their section of the sign that week for every passing car to see.

Forced creativity, as well as the need to work in teams, is good for kids. Our goal is for the school to quickly develop a reputation for creative thought and action. The ever-changing symbols in front of the school will bear witness to the commitment to remain active and to always be a forward-thinking institution. Over time we expect people will pass the school often to see the new design, colors, and to read the names of the students responsible for the creativity of the sign. Research will tell us the impact that this has on the school community and the community at large.

Student Companies on Campus

Student-run organizations are where students learn what it is like to manage a coffee shop, or the campus store, or operate a day care center for staff and the community. Students learn about supply and demand, operating costs, projections, budgeting, marketing; everything involved in running a company becomes accessible to the interested student. In these cases, students demonstrate their understanding of math, for example, by papers they write, describing their engagement in the store or coffee shop.

If one of the student companies has a coffee-shop business or serves lunch, there is a place to advertise that service to the neighborhood on the school sign.

The Entrance Area

The entrance area celebrates the students' work. Each student is represented by a picture and a short bio with an aspirational quote from the student to themselves in ten years.

This space also serves as an inviting gathering place for students, with comfortable furniture and a wall of monitors showing the latest videos created by students. On one side is the entrance to the school store, the public restaurant or coffee room, and the day care center. This area should be a cross between the Apple Store and the Two Bit Circus with bright, exciting, positive music, daylight, and plants, along with the latest technology.

The school store, cafeteria, and restaurant can share the same space—a 25-foot-by-50-foot room next to the kitchen, ideally with an outside seating area for use in good weather. This allows for seating for 40 customers.

The Student Store

This store, in addition to T-shirts and the typical swag that a school sells, is stocked with products and art created by the students.

The Day Care Center

This would require a 15-foot-by-30-foot space with its own separate outside play area. The student corporations manage these facilities on the campus with appropriate educators and adults to comply with regulations. The availability of a day care center helps the school in several ways. It becomes a powerful recruitment tool for the kind of teachers we want teaching our kids, and it offers the students an experience of working with young children. Also, the students set pricing for faculty as well as all nonfaculty families.

FEW CLASSROOMS

The school is open and unstructured. Kids can be walking around talking to friends, working on projects in the STEAM Lab Makerspace, or taking a nap in the nap room. The key is that the module-based reward system keeps us informed on students' progress. We know when to encourage a student to take a break and play or when to encourage a student to take hold of a situation and bear down and get to the other side of the problem.

Cubicle Rooms

Ideally, this room contains cubicles—one per student—each with a locker, bookshelf, lighting, and places for personal decoration. In areas that have limited budgets, these cubicles can be "hot bunked," with two kids sharing one cubicle at different times, as they engage in other areas or use the open collaborative space. They sign up for their time needed in the cubicle.

Each cubicle has an L-shaped workstation that the student will use as their home base. A large 27-inch flat-screen monitor is integral with the workstation. The computer screen is activated with a fingerprint scan and opens to the day's news. Software modules deliver the curriculum, and the teacher monitors the progress. There is a teacher nearby, but the teacher is sitting in his or her own cubicle when there are many students taking lessons.

Teachers are on a connected device that alerts them if additional teachers are needed for lesson support. When in the teacher cubicle, the teacher can intervene by way of a videoconference at any point. Any student can ask for assistance using the same system. A diligent student can finish the day's modules in two to three hours—any three hours during the day.

Sometimes when a student is really on a roll with a subject, they may wish to complete five modules in a day. That same student may decide to do none the next day. Lack of forced time and structure drives many teachers and parents crazy. But kids love the freedom of self-determination and find that it changes their attitude about the process. Chuck E. Cheese taught us a great deal about what kids like, and it is seldom what adults like.

Students are allowed great freedom if they have enough $Eds in their account. It is an indirect reward system. Students earn them for accomplishments, and how they use them is within their control. $Eds mean the freedom to self-determine how free hours in the days are spent, and many of the pleasures on campus will be available by spending $Eds.

Classrooms

There is a need for two or three classrooms for every 300 students. Two are with an oval table and 12 chairs surrounded by chalkboards. Each classroom also has a mentor's console. The students are in front of two projection screens with feedback systems. Quick math will tell you that kids will spend less than 7 percent of their time in a classroom, and when they do, it will be in a tiny class compared with the size of classes today.

There would be some small classrooms where kids can sit around a table and explore ideas together, with or without the teacher's supervision or leadership. The schedule of these meetings is posted in public spaces around campus, and students are invited to attend if they have an interest in that particular topic. They do get $Eds for attending. No punishment for not attending.

The physical space is constantly changing to accommodate collaborative projects. The workstations are mobile and can be clustered into workgroups.

Each school would have a theater to provide space to allow for student presentations, movies, and guest speakers.

Student Workout Stations

We would encourage treadmill desks, Dance Dance Revolution (DDR) workout stations, and stationary bikes with terminals; weight machines would also be available. All machines are connected to the network, and all can be monitored and controlled by software. Each student would be required to pick an activity and engage in that for at least 40 minutes per day. This can be dancing, running, walking, lifting weights, or any physical activity the student is interested in and can be monitored while taking part.

Nap Rooms

It has been shown that a 20-minute nap in the afternoon can drastically improve performance. We supply the darkened space with mats to make it possible and encourage students to take advantage of it. Along each wall, we can hang bunks five feet high and two feet wide with mats. The capacity of most nap rooms would be approximately 50. Two of these rooms would be placed adjacent to the shower rooms—one for boys and one for girls.

Group Rooms

This would be a large space whose distinctive feature is a huge map of the world that covers the floor. The room is 70 feet by 40 feet, which makes the distance between California and New York about 15 feet. All walls are covered with blackboard paint; one includes a calendar that has the month's events posted by the students. The other shows a time line of history. The third will be for free-form writing, perhaps with the poem of the week in a special space, and graffiti art.

At one end is an open kitchen that is staffed with students and a mentor chef.

There are tables and chairs, beanbag chairs, and pillows. There would be lighted cubby spaces for personal items to be stored.

The STEAM Lab Makerspace

The STEAM Lab Makerspace is where a lot of the fun takes place. There are large project tables, lockers to store projects, and a series of spaces that have specialized equipment that can be used for projects. This equipment includes a laser cutter, CNC router, electronics lab, power tools, a greenhouse, ceramics kiln, chemistry hood, DNA sequencer, soundproof music-practice rooms, a small sound stage, a green screen, music synthesizing and editing capability, and a video editing suite. The objective is to have enough equipment to allow maximum creative expression and exploration. The equipment can be bought used and is often surprisingly cheap. The whole facility equipment budget is $150,000.

The STEAM Lab Makerspace is part of the reward structure and can only be accessed with $Eds after a sufficient number of modules have been completed.

Company Rooms

There are at least 20 student-run companies that can be easily identified and managed by student groups. There would be rooms for each company, with any needed equipment. For example, the company room for the waste management company would include white boards for planning and space for testing composting and recycling projects. It will look different from the room used by a group engaged in product development.

Gym

One option would be to have a gymnasium that allows for team sports, especially for high schools. Otherwise, exercise rooms provide much-needed cardiovascular workouts. The availability of a sports facility is beneficial as an added way to get kids moving. Some kids will join teams; some will be there to dance.

The gym will also look and feel creative, with art hanging from the ceiling. Some of the art will be high-tech, some might be watercolors; most of it will be created by students. Often creativity is linked with the arts, and although that is a place where we see great exhibits of creative work, creativity is needed in every discipline, including physical exercise.

BUILDING CREATIVITY INTO THE ENTIRE SPACE

There are many forms of creativity, and creative problem-solving is a skill that will become more and more important in a future that promises a myriad of challenges to our environment and our economic stability. The issues of fostering creativity have many possible answers. One is to have creativity built into the DNA of the environment. Creativity gives birth to additional creativity. If it is invited and encouraged, it will thrive.

There are several theories on creativity that will be implemented. The first and easiest is to lower the risk. Creators need to be able to fail. Fear of failure is the most stifling influence on new ideas. Our current public schools inadvertently reinforce the concept that there is a right and wrong answer to anything. Very few foster the concept that in many situations there are multiple right answers.

With one of our companies, we rented a horrible facility that needed a total reformation. We decided that we would paint most of the walls with blackboard paint. Then we placed chalk and erasers every 10 feet and told everyone that they were free to create anything they wanted. Quickly the facility came alive. What was a cheap fix for the building created a rich look and feel. The impermanence of the drawings and messages gave everyone the courage to play. Quickly the wall across from the restrooms became the company calendar, and though there was an online schedule, the constant reminder of deadlines and the ability to anonymously comment on them led to tremendous feedback. The favorite comment format was a text bubble attached to an issue or graphic.

Offices and the walls around the door started with just the name of the occupant but soon expanded to include comments about the occupant and birthday greetings and congratulations about a new relationship. It gave everyone an opportunity to play.

One very good outcome was increased activity on deadlines that were slipping. In most cases we were able to shift people around early enough that a project could still come in on time.

HAVING FUN CAN TEACH COOPERATION

Pranks and play may be a precursor to creative thinking and be necessary in a creative individual. In a company or a school, people pranking and playing leads to a fun and creative corporate culture. Let everyone know that it is okay to play. The parameters are pretty simple: Ask yourself is it kind to all involved? If the answer is yes, have at it. If there is a victim, however, that prank is out.

It should be noted that many super innovations were considered at their inception as a toy or hobby. The automobile and airplanes are the most common examples. At their inception they were considered playthings for the rich. Video games ushered in the cultural shift to personal computers. Everyone thought that video games were a waste of time. Many still do. But there are plenty of multimillionaires in the tech industry who would argue the point with some merit.

There was a high correlation in the early 1980s between programming and video games. Enough that several countries that restricted video game play found that they had low adoption of computers and programming skills. I know that my own kids made the leap from game playing to computer programming when I showed them how to create a Doom level. They were fascinated by the fact that they could place objects in this synthetic world and then go into that world and see and interact with the objects they placed there. All the kids in this school will learn how to do this simple feat. Will they all become programmers? No. But they will all have a greater understanding of the computer world and the creation of images and actions in a digital environment.

Here is a story I heard about a ceramics class that was split into two groups. One half of the group was told that they would only be graded on how many pots they created by weight. The second group was told that they would be graded on one pot that was as good as they could produce. The interesting outcome was that all the good pots were judged to come from the quantity group. It appeared that the act of doing many pots gave more creative freedom and allowed the students to experiment and to learn from trial and error.

Much of creativity comes from deviating from the norm. By nature, normal is not creative. Irreverence (which is part of pranks) may also be a part of truly creative endeavors. Our environment in the school will be rich in low-risk ways to create, and the campus will be rich in tools and materials. Play and playful learning will be encouraged as part of every day.

ExoDexa-powered campuses will be student focused and will offer an open invitation to be creative and leave your mark on your campus.

Often a design survives until it meets the real world. I expect that some of these ideas may not work or will have some unintended consequences. They always do. However, I think that number will be small. The issue is to be recursive as educators and also to fix what does not work. I hope that others will contribute new ideas and processes to make the learning even better, more relevant, and faster. It is the key to our society and our future.

By now many will be thinking that this school sounds very expensive, and our schools are broken and broke. All that computer equipment and networks, the STEAM Lab Makerspace equipment, and the teachers who supervise it—all that has to cost a great deal of money.

In structuring this school system, nothing has been added that cannot be inserted into a current school budget. There's some restructuring, of course, but we are confident that the money being spent per student in most districts can easily support this system.

THE BUSINESS OF RUNNING A SCHOOL

A shop-floor analysis says this: The best way to view any manufacturing process is to look at the unit economics of the product and to focus all on supporting that unit on the shop floor. If you think of a school as a factory that takes in raw material—kids—and finishes them into educated high school graduates, a high school looks much like a factory. In this model, the business community represents the consumer of the product. The better the product, the higher salary the student commands.

Administrative Costs

A high school classroom in Los Angeles has an average of 35 students, and the funding for each student is $9,600. If that classroom were a one-room schoolhouse, the school would have a $336,000 budget for the year. The average salary with benefits for a Los Angeles teacher is $60,000, and the cost of rent (or payments of purchasing) for the room, energy, maintenance, and janitorial services, is about $30,000. Books and materials can come in at $800 per student, or $28,000. Desks, chairs, and blackboards, if rented for the year, come to $2,000. The total cost is $120,000. Where does the other $216,000 go?

The quick answer is excessive administration. Most private companies have G&A (general and administrative costs) in the neighborhood of 5 percent. Some very efficient companies get it down to 2 or 3 percent. Some companies play games with classifications that obscure actual costs. School districts and states are much worse. Trying to find out exactly where the money goes in a school district is much harder than it would first appear. School districts should be required to provide quarterly reports that follow SEC requirements for public companies.

Automate Record Keeping and Payroll

The school should be designed to be an efficient user of labor and should aim to apply that labor where it can be most productive. It should outsource as much as possible to technology. For example, all the records of students' performance and attendance would happen automatically with no human interference. Since there are no letter grades, but simply an account of modules completed, the student transcript is always up to date and complete and can be made available to potential employers or universities easily by the student by assigning a password to the employer or organization. A simple computer algorithm can supply letter grades based on modules completed if the university or employer needs them.

The teachers' payroll is automated, and all repetitive billings like rent and energy are also automatic, with little human intervention. The headmaster on campus has no need for a secretary or staff and actually spends most of the time interacting with teachers and students. They may also teach and organize enrichment activities for staff and teachers. The fact that technology takes care of time-consuming, low-reward (for either the student or the teacher) tasks leaves the educator and the students room for a very different experience. The teacher is now an instigator, a collaborator, a mentor.

As in any effective organization, the teacher will bring in support as needed and send students for guidance when that is the appropriate next step. Having access to this kind of individualized education was a dream a decade ago. It's now technically possible, although not yet highly visible.

Give Teachers More Control over Spending

The cost of this education can be crafted based on extracurricular needs. Since most of the STEM subjects are taught by modules, the labor component encompasses the help given to kids who are struggling with a particular concept. The need for large numbers of educators for these subjects is driven by how long a student needs to wait for help or how active the teachers are in intervening with a struggling student. As the modules become broadly used, teachers will be available to spend more and more time coaching the students in the projects in the STEAM Lab Makerspace, the school companies, or on trips and functions outside the school.

A minimum school budget can be as little as $4,000 per student per year. That may mean that some of the STEAM Lab Makerspace equipment will be listed as aspirational, but many of the activities would still be available. If the school owns the facility, as is the case in many parochial and private schools and some charter schools, a very good education is available for $7,000 per student per year.

Several sample school budgets along with samples of per student costs can be found online.

WE CAN PROVE OUR WORTH

This plan for the ExoDexa-powered schools is radical, and radical change is scary to some people. Parents particularly are conservative when it comes to their children. They do not want to play dice with their kids' futures. We will rely on need and a compelling story until the research data is collected.

The best way to establish something new is to prove efficacy. If this system does not work exceptionally well, it does not deserve to be replicated; but if our results are as we calculate, we will blow the doors off standard tests and put the ExoDexa method up against the best private or public schools. Of course, we will prove efficacy through third-party evaluation of the research and the data.

There is such a huge demand for something different that many will try aspects of this program on faith and the desire for something that will engage their child more even before complete proof of efficacy is shown. The fact that a school can be started that is cheaper and better will draw many to the concepts that are easy to implement in existing schools.

The modules will be made available to anyone at a modest charge, and we expect that the early market will be from the homeschool community. Private and parochial schools will come next, with the public schools coming last. Growth will be steady and based on our franchise program.

OUR FRANCHISE PROGRAM

Franchises are an effective model for deploying a business. The franchisor provides methods, equipment, training, and a guarantee of quality. There is also a collective marketing plan in which all participate and benefit. The name becomes a standard of excellence that becomes a guarantee of quality control and effectiveness. At Chuck E. Cheese we put hundreds of managers through training and helped with store layouts and real-estate selection and provided hard-to-obtain equipment at better prices than could be individually sourced.

It was a turnkey solution with a known outcome, and the company's growth exploded. If we can truly prove learning outcomes that are 20 percent better for the same money as conventional schools, we will dominate the market in as little as three years. Think of all the private schools that spend $20,000 to $50,000 per student and have only slightly better outcomes than public schools. Our $7,000 per student will be hard to believe. Bare-bones schools set up in churches for a cost of $4,000 per student will also be offered that represent a franchise lite.

Not all will want to be a franchisor. Some may choose instead to take part of the system, such as the remote specialist mentors and the modules. Perhaps they will use some of the integrated learning without access to things like exercise machines. Some will obtain very good outcomes with just those shifts. Over time I think these schools will adapt more and more of the whole program and perhaps choose to franchise later. Let's engage interested parties on whatever scale makes sense to get started. Efficacy will breed a desire for deeper engagement.

As we build out the international curriculum, we will appoint master franchisors in each country because of the unique issues of regulation and licensing that each nation presents. Many countries do not allow as many freedoms as the US.

I truly believe that most teachers want to see change, but they have one question: What if the change means I lose my job? None of the fear of this bad outcome needs to be of concern. There are simply not enough good teachers. I think the most interesting thing that will happen in the next few years will be the way that radical change comes to the bureaucracy. I expect a fight.

Extracting Immediate Feedback

The ExoDexa structure will yield a massive amount of data that can be used to better understand how kids learn and the mind-body links that are already known but have been the subject of little research.

The nature of the modules and the bite-size information and testing give immediate feedback about the time of cognition and the speed of mastery. With a few extra steps that define a student's state of health, nutrition, psychological profile, and other factors that affect learning, we should be able to start truly understanding this massively complex issue.

We will create the environment for much of this research ourselves and offer our schools to universities all over the world as a laboratory for research on the mind-body connection, performance, and attention, and we will be uniquely situated to perform tests.

See the Appendix for examples of topics for future study.

RETHINKING BIG

Nolan is rethinking everything about how we educate students—from curriculum to the physical space.

By gamifying curriculum, individualizing learning programs into what he is referring to as "modules," and redesigning the physical school, Nolan's concept could make schools more creative, collaborative, and inviting.

Nolan asked if some students might think better when active. What would Gillian Lynne, who went from fidgety student to world-class choreographer, say to that? What would the principal who came up with the idea of a dance class rather than a psychiatrist recommend here? Yes, some kids need to be moving to process and learn. Having a system in which to measure impact in real time was not possible a decade ago.

Many public schools in large cities are tired looking. The paint is old, the floors are old, and the fence is fit for a detention center. Worst of all, the buildings are locked up after school and over the weekend. Their playgrounds are not part of the community, except when school is in session. That seems like a waste of assets and a lost opportunity to have the students feel at home and welcome on campus. In an effective educational setting, students should feel like campus is an inviting part of their community experience.

Nolan posits that most schools can be made to fit this new concept with little expense. I'm not an expert on the structure or finances of education. I do understand the impact possible for students' education. I believe that everything Nolan has proposed in this book will inspire the children lucky enough to engage in the ExoDexa system, and it will offer a system ready for academic research to confirm the hypothesis.

Conclusion

I have had fun writing this book. Doing research is fun when trying to understand something, though it can also be depressing when a picture emerges that contrasts what should be great with what currently is horrible. It is doubly depressing if the area is important for the lives and happiness of so many people and the children of the world. The best antidotes for depression are action and hope. This book is our action, and it gives rise to the hope that we can make things better and soon. Ideas have power, and vetted ideas have superpower. Yes, I believe that we can change the world.

If you have taken the time to read this book, by now you have an opinion as an advocate or critic. Either is great, because we need all the allies we can get, and we also welcome criticism and input on ways we can improve. Perfection is a long road and a group effort; all those of goodwill are encouraged to participate either way.

YOUR ACTION ITEMS

- Give your copy of the book away. Send an e-book copy to all your friends. Talk about fixing education to friends and family, and talk about ideas that can make things better. Vote and support the local school boards. Be an advocate for change.

- Reread the St. Crispin's Day speech from Shakespeare's *Henry V.* Become part of the Band of Brothers (or sisters) and pity those who did not join our quest. We have lives to save.

- Become a ExoDexa shareholder. Perhaps you can make a profit while being an advocate. It is okay to do well while doing good.

—Nolan

Appendix

TOPICS FOR FUTURE STUDY

Some of the topics for research are listed below, but this list is far from complete.

Exercise and Learning

We know that vigorous exercise before learning is beneficial, but what we do not know is the optimum exercise amount or duration. We do not know if it is universally important for all students or for certain learning types in particular.

Heart Rate and Learning

Tracking a student's heart rate over the day and matching that to learning will be instructive. Do some kids learn better when slightly active? Do kids who fidget do better if they are moving? We know that many like to think while pacing. Do some kids learn better while on a treadmill desk and simply raising their heart rate 10 or 20 beats per minute? The idea of walking while learning may have surprising results.

Nutrition and Learning

Is there a difference in learning if a student has a light carbohydrate breakfast, a large carbohydrate breakfast, or a protein breakfast? By feeding kids in the morning and providing a measured breakfast, the answers should become evident. Not all kids may respond the same way.

Snacks and Learning

Two hours after breakfast, many kids want a snack. What is best for their mental acuity? Which is the best: protein or carbohydrates? We know that the brain burns a lot of energy. A dive into the research that exists will inform our approach, and we will encourage more research on this topic.

Morning vs. Afternoon Learning

We know that some students are morning people, and others function better in the afternoon. What can we learn about the causes and the proper tasking by the time of day? We all have circadian rhythms, and understanding these features on an individual basis should allow for better outcomes.

Stimulants and Learning

Most office workers are convinced that a cup of coffee or tea makes them more productive. Should kids be allowed to have a cup of tea or coffee at their workstations? In the case of ADHD, what is the actual effect of Ritalin or some of the other forms of amphetamines? Are there better ways to deal with hyperactivity? We have noticed that some children labeled with ADHD have no problem focusing when they are in a game they are drawn to. There is room for more research on this subject.

Home Environments and Learning

Some kids come from very troubled environments. We believe that we can cost effectively provide a partial boarding-school environment by using sleeping bags and nap rooms to give a 24-hour school experience five days a week. The parents drop off the child Monday morning and pick them up Friday afternoon. In this situation we can measure the effects of the learning when the child is in a uniform environment versus their toxic home environment. Perhaps, in the future, a full boarding school will be available in which to place our technology and further refine results.

Sleep and Learning

Sleep is important to health and learning, but how much is enough? Our kids will have constant heart-rate monitoring and a few other readouts, such as oxygen level and implied blood pressure. We can track sleeping and waking periods and gain insights about the links between them. As we expand the experiment, there are cheaper and easier EEG sensors that can be used for additional inputs.

Metabolism and Learning

Each student has a different metabolism, and their rate of burning energy is an indication of biological activity. Linking learning styles and cognition of material should lead to some interesting relationships. Stimulants tend to raise metabolism; perhaps we can divine a perfect metabolism for each student.

While there are probably a hundred more tests that can be set up and studied, the reality of knowing moment by moment when and how a child learns may be an important key to teaching at various speeds.

The Different Faces of IQ

If you can measure something, it becomes a tool that can be used for improving outcomes. By splitting out the component parts of IQ, we should be more effective in presenting appropriate modules to students who have particular gifts or particular difficulties. A significant study of this aspect of the mind may be crucial to creating solutions for students with a variety of learning challenges.

Index

A

ability to thrive, teaching, 121
accounting skills, 155
administrative costs, 233
Angelou, Maya, 35
Arduino boards, 69n7
art activities, 121
Atari, 7, 8
attention. *See also* student
   engagement
  competing for, 18–19
  monitoring, 104
attention deficit disorder, 19, 124
avatars, mentors' use of, 101–3

B

BDNF (brain-derived neurotrophic
   factor), 112
Beats by Me project, 49
bias in classroom, reducing, 82,
   90–94
Billings, Russell, 9
boredom, avoiding
  exploring interests, 80
  freedom from boredom, 71–73
  gamified approach to education,
   83
  learn-at-your-own-pace school,
   145

brain activity, optimizing, 110–13
brain-derived neurotrophic factor
   (BDNF), 112
Brain Rules (Medina), 61, 111, 129
Bridge program, Antioch University
   Los Angeles, 142
Bushnell, Brent, 29, 67
Bushnell kids, 66
Bushnell, Nolan, 5, 7–9
business skills and entrepreneurship,
   31–33, 63–64, 67, 73
  accounting, 155
  advertising, 153
  creating jobs vs. finding jobs,
   153–54
  $Eds program, 158–60
  incentives, 158–60
  intrinsic vs. extrinsic rewards,
   156–57
  Junior Achievement program,
   155–56
  Lemelson Foundation, 156
  marketing, 152–53
  Paradigm Challenge event, 156
  paying kids for school work, 157
  resilience, 151
  transcripts and modules, 161–63
Buzan, Tony, 92, 147

C

Chuck E. Cheese, 7, 23, 158, 227, 236
classroom experiences. *See also* user experiences
  ExoDexa system, 227
  school of the future, 3–5
  traditional/typical, 2
coaching, online, 34, 97
collaboration among students, 49–50, 57
college degrees
  creative thinking and, 31–32
  global economy and, 31
communication skills, 139–40, 142–44
company rooms, ExoDexa school, 229
confidence, building
  with game design, 133–34, 150
  group study, 114
  overcoming fear of failure, 15, 133
  partnering students, 57
  by prioritizing interests and talents of student, 150
  self-directed learning and, 168–70
coping skills
  enthusiasm and creativity and, 130
  learning from failures and setbacks, 66–67, 76–77
COVID-19
  impact on healthy habits, 58
  lessons learned from, 64–65
  pre-existing health issues and, 108
creating jobs vs. finding jobs, 153–54
creative thinking
  college degrees and, 31–32
  cultivating, 29–31
  importance of teaching, 15–17
creativity. *See also* enthusiasm and creativity; gamified approach to education

building into space, 230–32
optimism and enthusiasm and, 75–76
cubicle rooms, ExoDexa system, 226–27
curiosity, inspiring, 46–47

D

Dalai Lama, 191
Dance Dance Revolution, 62
day care center, ExoDexa system, 225
Department of Innovation, LAUSD, 9
design, ExoDexa school building, 222–23
diet, 104–6, 242
digital curriculum. *See* ExoDexa system; gamified approach to education; learning modules
digital literacy, 134–35
Doe, Kelvin, 70–71
Doerrfeld, Cori, 57
"Do Schools Kill Creativity?" TED Talk (Robinson), 29, 53
Ducard, Malik, 72

E

eBay, 136
ED Games Expo, 17
$Eds program, 105–106, 158–60, 183, 227, 229
Educational Testing Service, 128
education, approaches to. *See also* gamified approach to education
  business perspective, 14
  challenge of implementing changes to, 24–25
  effect of pandemic on, 13
  efficiency and, 21–22

inflation and, 25
one-to-many delivery method,
    30, 83
optimizing individual outcomes,
    27–28
politics and, 21–22
preparing students to become
    world citizens, 32–34
profit motive, 21
public vs private education, 24
social-emotional learning, 15–16
Two Bit Circus Foundation, 9,
    14–15
two-tier education system, 25
educators
    believing in student, 195
    benefits of using digital curricu-
        lum, 95–97
    engagement of, 94
    facilitating access to, 95–103
    motivation, 187
    one-to-many delivery methods,
        30, 83
    problem with seniority, 22
    as sounding boards, 36
    teacher-as-mentor role, 37, 90–91
"effective multitasking" myth, 109
efficiency, importance of, 21–22
engagement. See student engagement
enthusiasm and creativity
    art activities, 121
    contagious nature of, 129–30
    coping skills and, 130
    cultivating through game design,
        133–38
    discovering hidden talents, 126–27
    effect of accepted attitudes about
        education on, 128–29
    exercise and, 131
    healthy view of failures and set-
        backs, 123

inspiring life skills, 123–38
learning-by-doing approach,
    119–22
musical instruments, 120–21
as precursors to passion, 131–32
role in building confidence,
    132–33
scientific instruments, 119–20
searching for beauty, 132
tests disguised as games, 124–25
entrance area, ExoDexa system, 225
Erdynast, Albert, 115–16
escape rooms, 17
exceptional students
    role of mentors in helping, 37
    user experience, 204–7
exercise and learning
    enthusiasm and creativity and,
        131–32
    ExoDexa system, 221–22, 229–30
    healthy habits to promote engage-
        ment, 59, 61–62, 106, 110–14
    research, 241
ExoDexa system. See also user
    experiences
    access to educators and mentors,
        95–103
    administrative costs, 233
    automating record keeping and
        payroll, 234
    building creativity into space,
        230–32
    classrooms, 227
    company rooms, 229
    creating an environment to thrive,
        139–51
    cubicle rooms, 226–27
    day care center, 225
    $Eds program, 105-106, 158–60,
        227, 229
    emphasizing healthy habits, 104–9

entrance area, 225
extracting immediate feedback, 237
franchise program, 236–37
gamified approach to education, 80–90
group rooms, 228
group study, 113–17
gym, 229–30
inspiring life skills, 123–38
learning-by-doing, 119–22
meeting social needs of students, 35–38
mentor/tutoring network, 37–38
nap rooms, 228
no-homework policy, 161
online coaching, 34
optimizing brain activity, 110–13
overview, 80–81, 219–20
preparing students to become world citizens, 32–34
promoting business skills and entrepreneurship., 31–32, 152–63
proving efficacy of, 235–36
redesigned school building, 222–23
reducing bias in classroom with, 90–94
school day structure, 221–22
school sign, 223–24
STEAM Lab Makerspace, 229
strategies and tactics, 80–90
student companies on campus, 224
student store, 225
student workout stations, 228
extrinsic rewards, 156–57

F

failures and setbacks
healthy view of, 10, 123
learning from, 66–67, 76–77
overcoming fear of, 15
feedback, ExoDexa system, 237
Finding the Next Steve Jobs (Bushnell), 8
Ford, Henry, 76
foreign-language subjects, 32–33
franchise program, ExoDexa system, 236–37

G

G&A (general and administrative costs), 233
game design
building student confidence with, 150
cultivating enthusiasm and creativity through, 133–38
"game loop," 20
gamified approach to education, 88. *See also* ExoDexa system
"game loop," 20
learning modules, 81–94
overview, 17–18
reducing bias in classroom, 90–91
salting the mine, 92–94
smell-a-vision modules, 87
tests disguised as games, 19–20, 124–25
tracking progress, 91–92
using video games to set goals, 51
Gardner, Howard, 127–28
general and administrative costs (G&A), 233
Gladwell, Malcolm, 55
global economy
college degrees, 31

educational approaches and, 31–35
goals
  Beats by Me project, 49
  building movement into curriculum, 50, 53
  collaboration among students, 49–50
  identifying, 43–44
  inspiring curiosity, 46–47
  instilling love of learning, 48–49, 52
  measuring thinking ability, 41–43
  mentors' role in helping students reach, 44–45
  overview, 39–41
  project-based learning results, 48–49
  using technology to engage students, 45–46
  using video games to set, 51
Griffin, Tim, 59
group rooms, ExoDexa system, 228
group study, 113–17
growth mindset, 17
gym, ExoDexa system, 229–30

H

Hanes, Leah, 9–11
healthy habits to promote engagement
  diet, 104–6
  exercise and learning, 59, 61–62, 106, 110–14
  home life, 107–9
  sleep, 106–7, 109
heart rate and learning, 241
Heung, Sammy, 33
hierarchy of needs, 111
Hollyn, Norman, 188

home life
  Monday-to-Friday sleepover school, 107–8
  as predictor of outcome, 130
  promoting healthy habits, 108–9
  research, 243
Houghton Mifflin Harcourt, 128

I

incentives, value of, 59, 158–60
inflation, educational approaches and, 25
interest and curiosity. *See also* student engagement
  exploring interests, 80
  freedom from boredom, 71–73
  interest-area modules, 142
  learning-by-doing approach, 67–71
  overview, 55–56
intrinsic rewards, 156–57
Invent to Learn (Martinez and Stager), 69, 129
IQ research, 244

J

Jobs, Steve, 7
Junior Achievement program, 65, 155–56

K

Khan Academy, 73
Khan, Sal, 73

L

LA Makerspace, 219
language training, 32–33

LAUSD (Los Angeles Unified
    School District), 9
Lean Forward Moment, The (Hollyn),
    188
learning-by-doing approach, 67–71
    role in promoting optimism and
        enthusiasm, 77
    with tools and instruments,
        119–22
learning modules
    avoiding boredom, 83
    collecting research data, 82, 87
    engaging multiple senses, 86–88
    15-minute duration, 86
    flexibility of, 83, 85
    overview, 81–82
    reducing bias in classroom with,
        90–94
    review system, 84–85
    role in lifelong learning, 84
    salting the mine, 92–94
    SLMs and, 88–89
    smell-a-vision modules, 87–88
    supporting teacher-as-mentor
        role, 90–91
    tracking student's progress, 84, 86,
        91–92
    trinkets, 171
learning through game play. *See*
    gamified approach to education
Lee, Bauer, 135
Lee, Connor, 135
Lemelson Foundation, 156
life skills, inspiring, 123–25. *See also*
    enthusiasm and creativity
listening to students, importance of,
    56–58
Los Angeles Unified School District
    (LAUSD), 9
love of learning, instilling, 48–49, 52
Lynne, Gillian, 53, 97

M

maker movement, 136
Martinez, Sylvia Libow, 69
Maslow, Abraham, 111
McGraw-Hill, 128
McLuhan, Marshall, 18
Medina, John, 61, 111, 129
mental health issues, 33
mental plasticity, 110
mentors
    facilitating access to, 95–103
    one-on-one mentoring, 98–99
    role in helping student reach goals,
        44–45
    teacher-as-mentor role, 37, 90–91
    use of avatars, 101–3
metabolism and learning, 243
mind mapping, 92
Monday-to-Friday sleepover school,
    107–8, 131
morning vs. afternoon learning, 242
movement, building into curriculum,
    50, 59–61, 110–13. *See also*
    exercise and learning
multitasking, 109
musical instruments, 120–21
music, using in curriculum, 59–60

N

nap rooms, ExoDexa system, 228
neurogenesis, 110–13
no-homework policy, 161
noise-canceling headsets, 88
nutrition and learning, 104–6, 242

O

one-on-one learning, 96, 98–99, 168,
    177
one-to-many delivery method, 30, 83

online learning. *See also* gamified approach to education
    coaching, 34
    digital literacy, 134–35
    foreign-language subjects, 32–33
optimism and enthusiasm. *See also* student engagement
    creativity and, 75–76
    exploring interests, 80
    identifying talents, 78–79
    learning-by-doing approach, 77
    learning from failures and setbacks, 76–77
    reducing bias in classroom, 90–94
Outliers (Gladwell), 55, 141

P

Paradigm Challenge event, 156
passion
    enthusiasm and creativity as precursors to, 131–32
    maker movement and, 136–37
payroll, automating, 234
Pearson Education, 128
peer-to-peer learning, 115
politics, educational approaches and, 21–22
practice principle, 141
problem-solving skills. *See also* gamified approach to education
    creativity and, 230–32
    escape rooms, 17
    importance of teaching, 15–17, 26
    learning-by-doing approach, 67–71
product, defined, 6
profit motive, educational approaches and, 21
project-based learning results, 48–49
public speaking, 114–15

public vs private education, 24
punch-card theory, 93

R

Rabbit Listened, The (Doerrfeld), 57
Ratey, John J., 111–12
reading skills, 139–44
record keeping, automating, 234
Reggio, Emilia, 79
research topics
    exercise and learning, 241
    heart rate and learning, 241
    home environments and learning, 243
    IQ, 244
    metabolism and learning, 243
    morning vs. afternoon learning, 242
    nutrition and learning, 242
    sleep and learning, 243
    snacks and learning, 242
    stimulants and learning, 242
review system, learning modules, 84–85
Robinson, Ken, 29, 53, 75, 79, 97

S

Sagan, Carl, 7
salting the mine, 92–94
school day structure, ExoDexa system, 221–22
school of the future. *See also* ExoDexa system; learning modules; user experiences
    classroom experiences, 3–5
    goals for, 40
school sign, ExoDexa system, 223–24
Schwartz, Tony, 109, 111

scientific instruments, 119–20
screen time, 144–46
self-directed learning. *See also* learn-
    ing modules
  in classroom with other students,
    88
  goals and, 43–44
  mentors and, 44–45
  student self-confidence and,
    168–70
Senderens, Alain, 137
sleep and learning, 106–7, 109, 243
SLMs (STEAM Lab Makerspaces),
    9, 88–89, 196, 229
small-group discussions (small-
    group practice), 114–17
smell-a-vision modules, 87
snacks and learning, 242
social-emotional learning, 15–16
Spare Parts (film), 70
Spark (Ratey), 111–12
Stager, Gary, 69, 129
STEAM Lab Makerspaces (SLMs),
    9, 88–89, 229
STEAM programs, 9
stimulants and learning, 242
Strauss, Valerie, 128
student-centered schedules, 146–51
student companies on campus, Exo-
    Dexa system, 224
student engagement. *See also* enthu-
    siasm and creativity; interest
    and curiosity
  avoiding boredom, 71–73, 83, 145
  Bushnell kids, 66
  business skills and entrepreneur-
    ship and, 63–64, 67, 73, 151–63
  communication skills and, 139–40,
    142–44
  healthy habits to promote, 58–59,
    61–62, 104–9
  importance of listening to stu-
    dents, 56–58

keeping kids motivated, 98–100
  learning from failures and set-
    backs, 66–67
  learning modules, 81–94
  movement, building into curricu-
    lum, 59–61
  one-on-one mentoring, 98–99
  practice principle, 141
  screen time, 144–46
  student-centered schedules,
    146–51
  students as productive members of
    society, 64–65
  of teachers, 94
  teaching problem-solving skills,
    67–71
  using music in curriculum, 59–60
  value of incentives, 59
  writing and reading skills, 139–44
students as productive members of
    society, 64–65
student store, ExoDexa system, 225

T

talent, identifying, 78–79, 126–27
teachers. *See* educators
technology, using to engage students,
    45–46
teenage suicide, 33
tests disguised as games, 19–20,
    124–25
text-only lessons, 86
thinking ability, measuring, 41–43
This Week in Asia (newspaper), 33
Torrez, Darlene, 9
transcripts and modules, 161–63
Trash for Teaching, 219
trinkets, 171
Two Bit Circus Foundation (2BCF),
    9, 14–15, 29, 77, 219
two-tier education system, 25

U

user experiences (user stories)
 confused teen, 203
 curious student, 169–70
 defined, 6
 emerging director, 187–88
 entrepreneur, 198–202, 215–17
 exceptional student, 204–7
 fashionista, 195–98
 foreign language student, 170–71
 former gangbanger, 172–77
 headmaster, 209–15
 high school history teacher, 165–68
 learning Chinese while exercising, 179–84
 mom of troubled youth, 191–94
 pastor, 207–8
 researcher, 217–19
 robot creator and designer, 189–90
 science teacher, 185–87

W

Waldorf education, 79
Way We're Working Isn't Working, The (Schwartz), 109
workout stations, ExoDexa system, 228
world citizens, preparing students to become, 32–34
writing skills, 139–43

Y

YouTube, 115, 120, 153

About the Authors

Nolan Bushnell

In 1972, Nolan Bushnell created an industry when he founded Atari and gave the world Pong, the first blockbuster video game. Today his design credo—that games should be "easy to learn and difficult to master"—is inspiring a new generation of developers. A prolific entrepreneur, Bushnell has started more than 20 companies, including Chuck E. Cheese's Pizza Time Theater; Catalyst Technologies, the first Silicon Valley incubator; and Etak, the first in-car navigation system. In the process, he pioneered many of the workplace innovations that have made Silicon Valley a long-standing magnet for creative talent. Bushnell was the first and only person ever to hire Steve Jobs, which he details in his 2013 book, *Finding the Next Steve Jobs*.

He is currently chairman of ExoDexa, a gamified education company; CKO of Moxy, a "play to earn" game and token platform; and an advisor to companies in the gaming and eSports spaces. Additionally, he sits on several boards, focusing on games, gaming, and robotics.

A true icon of the digital revolution, Bushnell was named one of "50 People Who Changed America" by *Newsweek*. A biopic about Bushnell, tentatively titled "Atari," was acquired by Leonardo DiCaprio's production company and is in pre-production.

Leah Hanes, PhD

Leah Hanes, PhD, grew up on a working farm in rural Canada with an older brother and a younger sister. Her parents celebrated 65 years of marriage before her father passed. She attributes this time as part of a loving, supportive family with her ability to overcome obstacles and envision a better future for students.

She is CEO of the Two Bit Circus Foundation (2BCF). During her tenure, first as executive director and then CEO, 2BCF has developed a strong voice in the current STEAM education discourse.

Her organizational efforts included a complete rebranding while executing strategic mergers with other like-minded organizations. Bringing potent creative play allies like T4T.org, STEAM Carnival, Imagination.org, and LA Makerspace under the 2BCF big top helped increase both reach and impact in education.

In March 2020, Dr. Hanes led an organizational shift, executing virtual events in the ensuing months. These include a number of virtual firsts for funders like AT&T, The Annenberg Foundation, and the American Honda Foundation, alongside traditional 2BCF events like professional development for educators, coding game jams for kids, and cardboard challenges for the entire planet.

Prior to joining 2BCF, Dr. Hanes held a variety of positions focused on children and education. Most recently, she taught courses on adult developmental theory and ethics at Antioch University Los Angeles. Her PhD included a study of ethical decision-making and gender at Antioch University's Graduate School of Leadership and Change. Her MA is in organizational management.

She is the mother of two grown children, a son and a daughter, and has a 13-year-old granddaughter and a grandson who is 8.